GUILTY BY POPULAR DEMAND

TRUE CRIME HISTORY SERIES

Twilight of Innocence: The Disappearance of Beverly Potts
  James Jessen Badal
Tracks to Murder
  Jonathan Goodman
Terrorism for Self-Glorification: The Herostratos Syndrome
  Albert Borowitz
Ripperology: A Study of the World's First Serial Killer and a Literary Phenomenon
  Robin Odell
The Good-bye Door: The Incredible True Story of America's First Female Serial Killer to Die in the Chair
  Diana Britt Franklin
Murder on Several Occasions
  Jonathan Goodman
The Murder of Mary Bean and Other Stories
  Elizabeth A. De Wolfe
Lethal Witness: Sir Bernard Spilsbury, Honorary Pathologist
  Andrew Rose
Murder of a Journalist: The True Story of the Death of Donald Ring Mellett
  Thomas Crowl
Musical Mysteries: From Mozart to John Lennon
  Albert Borowitz
The Adventuress: Murder, Blackmail, and Confidence Games in the Gilded Age
  Virginia A. McConnell
Queen Victoria's Stalker: The Strange Case of the Boy Jones
  Jan Bondeson
Born to Lose: Stanley B. Hoss and the Crime Spree That Gripped a Nation
  James G. Hollock
Murder and Martial Justice: Spying and Retribution in World War II America
  Meredith Lentz Adams
The Christmas Murders: Classic Stories of True Crime
  Jonathan Goodman
The Supernatural Murders: Classic Stories of True Crime
  Jonathan Goodman
Guilty by Popular Demand: A True Story of Small-Town Injustice
  Bill Osinski

GUILTY

BY POPULAR DEMAND

A True Story of Small-Town Injustice

BILL OSINSKI

THE KENT STATE UNIVERSITY PRESS

Kent, Ohio

INTRODUCTION

Who killed Todd and Annette?

When I first arrived in Logan, Ohio, in the near-zero cold of an early January morning in 1984, I assumed the state of Ohio had discovered the answer to that question. It was the first day of the trial of Dale N. Johnston, the man charged with those two unspeakably savage murders, so I expected I'd soon be hearing some strong evidence against him. The case had been cloaked in the dark of fear and mystery for more than a year; now all would be brought into the light of the court of justice.

As a reporter covering the trial for the *Akron Beacon Journal,* I was there because I had a job to do. I had a reserved seat in the small second-floor court-room in the Hocking County Courthouse. I was a little unsettled, though, as I took my seat and saw the eager faces of the people packing the spectator section. What had compelled these people to line up outside before dawn? Were they really so anxious to hear the lurid details of how the boy and girl next door had been killed and butchered?

From the start, it was clear the investigators and prosecutors considered Johnston to be a violent sexual deviant. According to the state's theory of the crimes, he had conducted an incestuous relationship with his eighteen-year-old stepdaughter Annette and then killed her and her boyfriend Todd in a jealous rage. After shooting them, the state charged, Johnston had compounded the horror by dismembering and mutilating the corpses, dumping the torsos into the Hocking River at a spot less than a mile from that very courthouse, and, finally, burying the remaining body parts in the middle of a field of corn planted in a tract of river-bottom land.

I waited through nearly three weeks of trial testimony for the prosecutors to present evidence of how Johnston had committed these crimes. On the last day, I was still waiting. I listened as the trial prosecutor gave a histrionic and, I thought, totally nonsensical closing argument. As an unbiased professional observer, I remember thinking to myself, "It couldn't have happened that way." He ended his summation with the macabre statement: "Murder is the ultimate form of incest." To me, it was as if he were saying: "We suspect this man of molesting his stepdaughter, so he surely must have killed her." I was more than a little shocked when, in short order, the three judges hearing the case agreed with him and convicted Johnston.

I stayed on the case. Back in those days, investigative journalism was still a significant part of the newspaper business, and so my paper supported me in my desire to examine the case more closely. I was able to spend significant parts of the next two years working the story. I wrote a series of articles pointing out the weaknesses in the state's case, and I wrote a long article about another man who had been in the Logan area at the time of the murders—a convicted killer who specialized in dismembering his victims. I argued that he made a much better suspect than Johnston.

I left Ohio in 1987 for another reporting job in Florida, so I missed covering the next milestone in the case: Johnston's successful appeal of the verdict and his release from prison after five years on death row. I was not surprised to learn that Hocking County prosecutors refused to reopen the murder investigations, insisting that Johnston was really the killer. I was again shocked, however, when Johnston lost his civil suit for wrongful imprisonment, despite his presentation of new evidence that supported his alibi. The state of Ohio had prevailed, arguing that Johnston still might be guilty and so should not be compensated.

Around that time, I started working on the manuscript that ultimately became this book. The story was compelling, but the ending was too murky. I put the project aside and moved to Atlanta, where I spent the final sixteen of my thirty-six years as a newspaper journalist.

Many times during those years, I fell asleep at night wondering if I'd ever find out who had killed those two kids. I hold to the Christian belief that all is revealed when we pass from this life to the next, so I took some consolation in the hope the truth would ultimately be made known to me. The only hitch was, I'd have to die first.

Thankfully, I was still alive on an otherwise unremarkable day in 2008, when I received a phone call from a woman I hadn't heard from in nearly twenty years. "Hello, Precious!" said Dolly Shaner, one of my sources during my investigations of the Logan murders. Dolly is an effusive woman who moves quickly to familiarities with her friends, but there seemed to be an added note of joy in her voice. Her sources within police agencies in central Ohio had passed along some big news: there was something stirring in the long-cold case. Someone was going to be charged with the killings, she said, and that someone was not Dale Johnston.

The indictments were handed down in September of that year, and the names of the accused killers—Chester McKnight and Kenny Linscott—were totally unknown to me and to all my old sources back in Ohio. At a hastily called sentencing hearing in December, McKnight pleaded guilty to shooting Todd and Annette. He gave few details about the crimes in the short time he was on the witness stand, received an extra seventeen years on the prison sentence he was already serving, and went back to his cell.

It was time to resurrect the book. I started commuting to Ohio. Each trip yielded new information and raised more questions. This time around, however, people were finally ready to talk. What they told me made an already disturbing story even more so.

Back in the 1980s, despite being convinced of Johnston's innocence, I had to concede that the premise could legitimately be debated. Now, though, the state of Ohio had certified that someone else had committed the murders. This meant that I had to review the history of this case through the lens of a new truth—and through this glass, things looked even darker than they had before.

We now know who killed Todd and Annette. The answer, sadly, begs other questions. How could every level of the justice system fail so miserably? How could good, small-town folks cheer as an innocent man was sent off to be executed? Who framed Dale Johnston?

Bill Osinski
April 2012

– 1 –

DEATH STROLL

The reigning Miss Parade of the Hills semifinalist flounced out of the yellowish clapboard house, making sure the door slammed behind her. Annette Johnston sidestepped the porch clutter and sniffed as she passed the metallic-gold '67 Pontiac LeMans carefully draped in canvas and parked in the front yard. Her boyfriend and sort-of fiancé Todd Schultz kept saying he was going to restore it and enter it in classic car shows . . . someday. Well, Todd could keep his dreams hidden under a tarp, but not Annette. She was tired of letting herself go; she'd never let the dark roots of her hair grow out so far.

That very day, Monday, October 4, 1982, Annette had received an A in her computer programming class at Hocking Technical College. She was a lock to get into Ohio State next year. Not long after she returned in midafternoon from the campus to the Schultz home, though, her pleasant mood deflated like a slashed car tire. She'd barely finished a sandwich before she and Todd got into it again.

Their fights were over matters so predictable they were almost boring. Todd kept whining about how she should drop out of school and marry him. Todd wanted her to pester her mother and stepfather, Sarah and Dale Johnston, to give her the orange Buick Skyhawk that they'd promised for her graduation, but still had not delivered nearly five months later. Todd had been a well-liked goofball in high school but, at age nineteen, he seemed to be increasingly comfortable with long-term unemployment. He'd lost his job at the mayor's print shop due to a hernia he suffered from the lifting and then lost his workers' compensation claim. Todd threatened to kill himself if Annette left him.

For Todd, that day had been another rotten one. He'd set out to address his two top priorities: an apartment for him and Annette and some quick cash. He'd failed on both fronts. He went to talk to his father, Don, about helping to get them into their own place, but Don offered sympathy without solutions. Then he went to discuss the matter of the ungifted Skyhawk with Will Kernan, a next-door neighbor and an attorney. Was there any way to force the Johnstons to give Annette the car? Their reason for the delay—that Sarah's only alternative would be to drive a rusted-out Pinto and that Annette would get the Skyhawk as soon as Dale started getting his expected royalty checks from leasing some of his land to a strip-mine operator—didn't seem, to Todd at least, to be good enough to renege on a promise. Kernan explained that a parent-child promise, though perhaps morally compelling, was not legally binding. Todd had been counting on converting the Skyhawk into a quick $1,000. He didn't know, because Annette didn't tell him, that she had more than twice that much in her savings account.

Todd never said why he needed the money, but it was obvious why he wanted his own apartment. He wanted sex with Annette like a hungry baby wants milk. When Annette moved out of her house and into the Schultz home two months earlier, Todd's mother Sandy seemed to be cool with the sex thing. At first, she told them they could have sex whenever Todd's little brother and sister weren't around. But in Annette's view, Sandy had lately become a queen-sized hemorrhoid about it, pitching a fit whenever she caught them screwing. Don was a bit more flexible. Recently divorced from Sandy, Don kept an apartment in town near the fire station where he worked, and he let Todd and Annette use it whenever he was on duty.

Annette liked sex just as much as the next girl. Probably more. Probably a lot more. But, really, was sex with Todd worth what it was costing her? Hadn't she just traded one set of shackles for another? Annette had told her mom she might be coming back home soon. She'd about had it with being a presumptive member of the Schultz family, and Sandy had told her she'd have to move out soon anyway. The welfare folks had told Sandy she couldn't have another adult in her household while she was accepting benefits for being separated from her husband. In any case, Annette had just about had it with Todd, and she'd definitely had it with Logan, Ohio, the bleak little mined-out Appalachian coal town where they lived.

Annette's noisy exit from the house on Henrietta Street broke Sandy Schultz's concentration on her studies for a tax-preparation course she was taking. She quickly learned from one of her younger children that Todd and Annette had been fighting. Then she went upstairs and found Todd lying on his bed, his elbows out and his hands behind his head, staring at the ceiling. She told Todd that Annette had just run off. Todd shook out of his pout and bounded after Annette.

He caught up with her about two blocks up where Henrietta hit Gallagher Street. Clara Anderson and her tenant George Groves were sitting on the front porch of her home near the intersection. They watched as the young couple had an emotional conversation that lasted about ten minutes.

"They had a little lovers' quarrel, I suppose," Clara said later.

It was clear to Clara that Todd and Annette had ended their fight successfully. They held hands and started walking off together down Gallagher toward Logan's industrial district. Todd draped his arm around Annette's shoulders, then turned and looked back down Henrietta. Sandy had come out of the house and was looking up the street. Todd waved to her, a signal that the magic of young love had been restored.

Todd and Annette were next seen a few blocks down Gallagher, near its intersection with Motherwell Street. They walked past a pickup stopped at a stop sign. The driver, Melody Morehouse, knew them both. Melody was fairly certain of the time. It was not long after the end of *General Hospital,* which would have been about 4:30. Melody was sure about that because after watching her favorite soap opera, she and two friends went out on a cigarette run. Melody tooted her horn, and Annette turned and waved. Then Melody saw the couple walking in the direction of the Home Tavern, where the city streets ended. Past the tavern, there was nothing but the Wolsky Stair Company factory and the tracks of the Chesapeake & Ohio Railway.

In those years, walking the C&O tracks was a common method of getting from Logan to West Logan on the opposite side of the Hocking River, whose dark green waters flowed so slowly in the fall that the only visible movement was of the leaves drifting on the surface.

A trestle bridge took the railroad tracks across the river. The train traffic was very light, and there was plenty of room for pedestrians to use the bridge. Its iron frame was rusted to a deep-red color, and the beams were decorated with spray-painted, time-faded proclamations of who loved whom and who was a slut. The stone abutments of the bridge on either side of the river made convenient steps for people to get down to the sloping riverbanks, thick with low-hanging tree limbs and underbrush. That section of riverbank was a popular spot for drinking, doing drugs, and having sex.

On the West Logan side, the tracks rose up about six feet from a triangular-shaped cornfield, a fifty- to sixty-acre piece of river bottom. The curving river formed the other two sides of the field, and farther on, State Highway 664 crossed both the river and the tracks.

Todd and Annette knew they wouldn't have much time to themselves as they walked the tracks. Todd was supposed to take his little brother Eric to soccer practice at about 6:00, and then he was to attend an auxiliary fire-fighters' meeting with his father.

The wooded banks of the Hocking River along the cornfield also served as a free campground for a small community of men who did not have, or did not want, homes. That day, one such man, Charles Blosser, saw a young couple having sex in a secluded spot on the banks. The woman had dark hair dyed blonde, like Annette, and the man had long, spindly legs, like Todd.

Having healed whatever emotional wounds that had caused their fight, Todd and Annette continued walking on the railroad tracks toward West Logan. A young man named Scott Cauthen saw them leave the tracks and go down a driveway leading into West Logan. They stopped at a garage sale, where they put down $5 to hold a coffee table. Apparently, they'd reached some agreement on new living arrangements. Then they proceeded to the home of someone they knew in West Logan, although this crucial bit of information did not come to light until many years later.

About a half hour later, at 5:45, give or take a minute or two, Charles Bartow, a part-time security guard at Armco Steel Company in the Logan industrial district, heard a noise from the direction of the cornfield. There were three gunshots, followed by a brief pause, then four or five more shots. Bartow was precise about the time, because 5:45 was when he was required to shut and lock the large doors of the warehouse. He was sure that he was on time that day, and just about certain the shots were fired by a .22-caliber weapon.

The drive-up window of the McDonald's on Hunter Street was just a few yards from the edge of the riverside cornfield. Rebecca Troops and Mary Cullison were stopped there at about 5:45, calling out their order, when they heard shots coming from the cornfield. They too were fairly certain the shots were fired by a .22.

At first, Shirley Frazier didn't think much about the confrontation on the railroad tracks she witnessed from the kitchen window of her mother's home on Homer Street in West Logan. Homer ran parallel to the C&O tracks, which were just twenty yards or so away from the back doors of the homes on the railroad side of the street. Frazier had much more serious things on her mind just then. Her estranged husband had come to the post office where she worked in Lancaster, about twenty miles north of Logan, dumped their two kids into her care, and took off. All she could do was bring them to her mother.

She was ranting to her mother about her no-good spouse when she saw a young blonde woman and a thin, brown-haired young man on the tracks, having an animated discussion with a taller, older man wearing dark-green coveralls and a hat of some kind. The older man seemed to be glowering at the couple. He went down the railroad track embankment and into the cornfield, followed by the younger man. The young woman seemed to become angry, and she walked down the embankment after them. Minutes later, Frazier was outside, loading her squawking kids into her car, when she heard three gunshots, probably fired by a .22. She heard a female voice calling out, "My God, you shot him!" Then several more shots and then silence. Moments later, the man in coveralls came up to the tracks from the cornfield side. He looked around and then looked straight at her. She got in the car and quickly drove off. At the time, she downplayed the significance of what she had seen. She'd grown up in that house on Homer Street; it wasn't uncommon to hear gunshots coming from the other side of the tracks. Gunplay was just one of the illicit pastimes people indulged in down there. Besides, she had her own crisis to deal with.

. . .

Back at the house on Henrietta Street, when 6:00 came but Todd did not, Sandy Schultz took Eric to soccer practice herself. Then, in an increasingly sour mood, she stopped off at Don's fire station, where she dropped off Eric's schoolbooks so that he could do his homework. She also deposited a piece of her mind with Don, telling him she didn't appreciate him making his apartment available for Todd's trysts with Annette. She figured that's where the couple had gone.

Sandy went to her tax class and returned home about 9:00 P.M. No Todd, no Annette, no Eric. She went to the fire station, where she at least found Eric; his coach had dropped him off. She was more angry than worried at this stage. She got a key to Don's apartment and marched off, fully prepared to spoil her son's romantic interlude. No one was there, and it didn't look as if anyone had been there that day. She took Eric home, but by now she was becoming more worried than angry.

She called the Johnstons' home and asked whether Todd and Annette were over there. Dale answered no, and Sandy hung up.

By the middle of that night, around 2:00 A.M., the corn moon, the first full moon of October, had risen like a golden opal over Logan. Sandy Schultz was finally falling asleep, but it was time for Clarence Mason to go to work. Mason lived on Homer Street in West Logan, and he worked as a night watchman at one of the plants in the industrial district. It was such a beautiful and clear night that Mason decided to walk the tracks to the plant. He walked through his backyard and up the embankment, but he stopped after taking only a few strides toward Logan. He heard some strange chanting, howling noises coming from the area near the trestle. This was one party that Mason was glad he hadn't been invited to. He turned back, got on his motorcycle, and drove the long way to work.

Down the block on Homer Street, Janice Moyer was up late. She was in the back upstairs bedroom, walking with the crying infant she'd recently taken in as a foster child. The window had a clear view of the access road that crossed the tracks and led into the cornfield. The access road allowed farm equipment to get into the cornfield and it was the only way to get a vehicle across the tracks.

In the middle of that night, Janice Moyer saw a strange parade going across the access road. There were three vehicles, traveling close enough to stay within each other's headlights. One was a dark-bodied pickup truck with a white roll bar, the second was another pickup with a yellow trail bike in the bed, and the third was a van.

What in the world, she wondered, were they doing driving into the cornfield at that hour? The corn was at least eight feet high, just about ready for harvest, so there was little room for the vehicles to maneuver down there. She was disturbed enough to wake up her husband Doug. He looked at the vehicles clustered below the access road in the cornfield and said, "There must be some wild party going on."

None of the people who saw or heard things in the vicinity of the railroad tracks or the cornfield that night—the garage-sale operator, Blosser, Bartow, Troops, Cullison, Frazier, Mason, Joyce and Doug Moyer—had any connection to any of the principals in the case. They all gave statements to the police—and they were all ignored.

Police investigators had to dismiss all the evidence that pointed to a crime in the cornfield because all those statements conflicted with the police theory of what happened to Todd and Annette. That theory was formed from a distraught mother's first suspicions, and police clung to it as monolithically as she did.

Sandy Schultz was desperate from the moment she woke up. She felt certain that Todd and Annette had been murdered, and she was just as certain that she knew who did it. She first voiced her convictions shortly after 9:00 the next morning, Tuesday, October 5, in the form of a phone call to the offices of Dr. Millard Mason, where Sarah Johnston worked as a receptionist.

"How could you live with such a pervert?" Sandy screeched when Sarah answered the phone. The shrill accusation almost drowned out Sandy's news that Todd and Annette were missing, but her diatribe would become the heart of the state's case and be echoed a year and a half later, in the prosecutor's final argument at the trial of Dale Johnston.

At this point, Sarah had no idea anything might be wrong. She was quickly disabused of that notion as Sandy continued her rant: I know what he did to Annette! She told me everything! Raping her, masturbating in front of her, touching her all the time!

Sarah had met Sandy only once before this phone call, when Sandy came with Todd on a rather uneventful visit to the Johnstons' home. There had been some tension between the two families due to Annette's move into the Schultz home, but never any open hostility and certainly never anything like the venom that was now being spat at Sarah.

As soon as she hung up, Sarah called Dale, who'd just come back home from feeding his livestock. He told her he'd go straightaway to the Schultzes' house and find out what was going on.

Dale knocked on the front door and then let himself in. Sandy was on the phone in the kitchen, and when she saw Dale she said into the phone, "The stepfather is here. Get over here."

"What's this about the kids being missing?" he asked.

Speaking to the man she now suspected of killing her son, she told him as much as she knew about Todd and Annette's departure and, more to the point, their failure to return.

Don Schultz entered the home and took over the interrogation. Have you seen the kids? Do you know where they might be?

No, Dale answered.

Don snarled that everybody in town knew what an asshole Dale was.

"We'll see who's the biggest asshole," Dale shot back.

"You know why she moved in here, don't you?" Don asked and then answered his own question. "It was because you couldn't keep your hands off her, that's why!"

Dale responded that Annette didn't exactly have a great track record when it came to telling the truth about her sexual exploits. If she told you that, he said, she must have thought it was what you wanted to hear. She was not an abused child, Dale insisted.

Don moved on to a litany of complaints about Annette. That girl had Todd wrapped around her little finger. Todd wouldn't even take the job Don had found for him in Columbus because he couldn't bear being away from his precious Annette. Todd even threatened to kill himself if he couldn't have Annette. Don didn't know where the kids were, but he was sure of one thing: That little bitch and her baggage would be out on the street the minute they showed up, he promised.

Dale started absorbing some of their fears. He left the Schultz home thinking that this might be more than two lovebirds running off together. He went back to Sarah's office and told her about the nasty allegations Sandy and Don had made against him.

"I don't care if you raped her every day of the week," Sarah said, within the hearing range of another office worker. "I just want my baby back in one piece."

That would never happen.

By the next day, October 6, the young couple had still not shown up, but their parents' tempers had cooled somewhat. Dale had a less hostile conversation with Sandy, and they found they agreed on something—that it might be a good idea to call in a psychic. Sandy believed there were people who possessed a sixth sense, and Dale believed he was one of them. Dale's mother had had "the gift," and in his dreams the previous night, Dale had seen a vision of Todd and Annette and water and trees.

Dale said he'd go to the nearby town of Haydenville to visit an old man named Raymond Mills, who claimed to be a seer. Dale had met Mills about a year earlier when Dale worked in a federal program to help elderly people keep their homes repaired. Mills had mentioned then that missing persons were a specialty of his.

First, Dale stopped at the Schultz home to pick up some of Annette's things to take to the old man. He selected some of her schoolbooks, her eyeglasses, her high school class ring, and a letter she'd written to a friend but had not yet mailed. He'd also brought along a picture of Annette. Sandy told Dale to add Annette's plastic container of birth control pills, since they meant so much to her.

The visit to the psychic provided Dale with a little ray of hope but no clear answers. The seventy-five-year-old Mills said he received only a flicker of a vision. He saw Todd and Annette walking together, and he saw some numbers: 1–0–6–5. Maybe the numbers were part of a license plate, maybe a street address. Perhaps Todd and Annette had run off to get married or to visit some friends, the old man said.

When Dale reported back to Sandy, he gave the most optimistic interpretation of the visit to the psychic, saying the old man believed the kids were still alive. Dale asked to take more of Annette's things, but Sandy refused, saying he should wait at least till the weekend. However, there was also a promising development to report from the realm of reality.

Don had reported the couple's disappearance on October 5, the morning after they'd gone missing. He had been told by a friend in the police department that later that same night, a sheriff's deputy in neighboring Fairfield County had been dispatched to the Buckeye Lake resort area to check out a report that Todd and Annette may have been seen there.

This was certainly worth checking out. Becky Hedges, the young woman to whom Annette had written the unmailed letter, lived on Buckeye Lake. Dale picked up Sarah, and they called the Hedges' home. Becky's mother told them she hadn't seen Todd and Annette, nor did she know anything about the deputy's visit.

Nevertheless, Dale and Sarah drove to the Hedges' home, where Mrs. Hedges told them the same thing she had told them over the phone. But if they wanted to talk to Becky, she'd be home in an hour or two.

The Johnstons used that time to drive to Lancaster, the Fairfield County seat. The sheriff's dispatcher searched the police logs and found an entry for Tuesday, October 5. The reporting deputy stated that Todd and Annette had been seen the previous night by Becky Hedges. That would have been the night they disappeared. Had Mrs. Hedges lied to them? They wouldn't be able to question the reporting deputy until he came on duty later that night.

Instead of waiting at the sheriff's office, they went around to some of the restaurants, gas stations, and boating supply shops that catered to the lake people, showing pictures of Annette and asking if anyone had seen her. All the responses were negative.

They returned to the Hedges' home, with Becky Hedges pulling in just ahead of them. Dale jumped out of his car, questioning Becky sharply before she could even exit. No, she said, she hadn't seen Annette since last Friday night's football game at Hocking County High. That's what she had told the deputy; he must have confused the dates on his report. Johnston realized that he'd become suspicious of Becky and her mother for no good reason. He apologized to them, and they understood. He called the sheriff's office and talked with the deputy who'd made the report. The error was confirmed, and the brief flicker of hope was extinguished. Now it was getting dark, time to give up for the day.

On Thursday, October 7, Dale had another seemingly promising lead to pursue. He remembered Annette telling him about one of her friends, Annette Farley, whose family had a cabin somewhere in the mountains of West

Virginia. It seemed like an ideal hiding place for runaway teens. Again, he went to Sandy Schultz for help. She got out a box of Annette's letters, and they found an address for the Farley cabin. Dale took the information to Logan Police Chief William Barron, but Barron told him Don Schultz had already told them about the cabin. The place had been checked out and found to be empty.

Nevertheless, Dale persisted. He made another round of calls to relatives, he went to places where he knew Todd and Annette had gone, and he ordered missing-person fliers with a picture of Annette from a local print shop. He went again to the psychic Mr. Mills, who cheered him up with a vision of Todd and Annette coming home. Mills added a troubling codicil— "Somebody's lying here." That was the only part of the old man's visions that turned out to be correct.

On the morning of Saturday, October 9, there was a final parental showdown. Dale and Sarah came to the Schultz home, hoping to collect the rest of Annette's belongings. They found Sandy morose and heavily medicated. Sarah was in only marginally better shape. As soon as they arrived, Sandy dispatched her son Eric to go next door to ask Cindy Kernan, Will's wife, to join them.

The meeting quickly took on the tone of a wake.

Todd's dead, Sandy announced. He was shot in the cornfield by the C&O tracks.

"Don't talk that way," Sarah said.

"I just know," Sandy moaned.

At about that time, Don Schultz was trying to confirm or disprove his wife's suspicions. He and his son Greg, Todd's older brother, and a few friends from the fire department were out searching the area of the railroad tracks, the riverbanks, and the cornfield. Don even looked in some empty boxcars. They found nothing.

Back at the Schultz home, Sandy said she was so sure that the worst had happened that she and Don had already discussed Todd's memorial. They decided they would restore Todd's pride-and-joy Pontiac, just the way he'd wanted. They would take it to the car shows, just like Todd would have. Sandy asked Cindy Kernan if they could rent space in the Kernans' garage to store the LeMans, once it was restored. Cindy said sure.

The talk about the car was a jab at some open wounds. It bothered Dale that Todd wouldn't let Annette get near his LeMans, while at the same time, Todd couldn't wait to get his hands on the Skyhawk that was coming to Annette. Todd loved his car more than he loved Annette, Dale said.

That wasn't true, Sandy shot back. Todd would surely have let Annette drive the LeMans, after he fixed it up.

Dale ended the conversational descent into melancholy by asking Cindy if he could speak to her privately. They went to the Kernans' house, where Dale told Cindy what the psychic had told him. He wasn't sure whether the information might upset Sandy, so he would let Cindy decide. Then he got to the real purpose of the conversation. What was going on in the Schultz home? Did Cindy know anything about the frequent fights that Annette had mentioned to Sarah? Cindy had nothing to share on those topics.

However, she did take the opportunity to tell him what she thought about his lifestyle. She repeated the same ugly allegations that Sandy had made. Apparently, what went on inside the Johnstons' trailer on Trowbridge Road was no longer limited to hearsay repeated by a distraught mother. It was the talk of the town. Cindy told him the widely accepted version of why Annette had moved out of her parents' home. It happened after Annette and Todd were changing into their swimsuits in the same room, and Dale gave them a good tongue-lashing. How could he be so hypocritical, Cindy asked, when everybody knew that Dale and Sarah paraded around their house naked and went skinny-dipping in their creek any time they felt like it?

All Dale could say is that kids are going to do what they're going to do, no matter what their parents say.

Sarah came then to get Dale. She wanted him to collect the rest of Annette's things and go home. All this talk was just making everybody even more miserable. Sandy's response to the Johnstons' request only made things worse.

"No. We haven't found them yet. Those things can stay here till we find them, and then you can have them," she said.

At that, Sarah ran out of the house, crying. Dale tried to comfort her and returned to the Schultz home to ask again for Annette's things. "That's all her Mommy has left of her," he pleaded. Sandy refused again. The next time the Johnstons and the Schultzes got together would be in the Hocking County Courthouse.

. . .

Set in the Appalachian foothills just east of where the land flattens into the great American plains, Logan, Ohio, will never be included in any back-roads guidebooks to scenic towns. It has no manicured town square. Gracious homes are hard to find. The downtown is anchored by the granite courthouse, a squat, two-story structure that is far from imposing. Visually, grey and green dominate the color palette of Logan. From winter through what passes for a spring, the sky, the trees, and even much of the ground are shades of grey; the greens of the trees and the grass get their turn in the short summer.

In the 1980s, as well as in present time, Main Street was, and is, pockmarked by boarded-up storefronts. Stagnation is a decades-old condition for Logan and for Hocking County. Census after census, the city's population has hovered slightly below seven thousand; the county's is near twenty thousand. Before World War II, Logan had a thriving glass factory and a shoe factory, but those are long gone. Coal mining carried the local economy for a while after the war, but that's just about gone, too. Tourists, though not many, come to see the fall color in the nearby Hocking Hills. Commuting to work in Columbus, thirty-five miles to the northeast, is not uncommon.

Logan's history as a town goes back to its founding in 1816. It was named for an Indian chief who was the son of an Indian mother and a French fur trader. Long after it was settled by people from the eastern states looking for land on the frontier of the Western Reserve, coal was discovered in the region. In New Straightsville, less than ten miles from Logan, the dangerous conditions in the mines led to the conflicts that helped form the United Mine Workers union. Labor protesters shoved a burning cart down a mineshaft in the early 1900s, and the resultant fire still burns today.

Still, as in most small towns, people know each other and care about each other in Logan. When two well-liked young people go missing, the loss is widely felt—as is the fear. About a month before the disappearance, some hunters in a neighboring county had found a garbage bag containing an unidentified man's carved-up corpse. Those sorts of things just are not supposed to happen in places like Logan.

Thus, it was the ordinary citizens of Logan who took the initiative in searching for Todd and Annette. On Tuesday, October 12, the local REACT (Radio Emergency Associated Citizens Team—a sort of volunteer police auxiliary) CB radio club organized a search of the area around the cornfield and the riverbanks. About a dozen club members gathered in the afternoon in the parking lot of an abandoned supermarket not far from the railroad tracks. The police had not yet made a systematic search of the area. The volunteers were not trying to show up the police. They were just using their common sense, which told them that two young lovers out for a walk don't run off and leave all their possessions behind.

They split up into small groups, one of which started walking the tracks. As they crossed the bridge, a woman volunteer pointed at something float-ing in the water, trapped in some debris. The men who were with her de-cided without going any closer that it probably wasn't anything human. The search was called off at dusk.

The REACT volunteers spread the word that they'd be searching the same area the next day. This time, Chief Barron decided that his department should be involved. He asked the editor of the *Logan Daily News* to put an item in the next day's paper, saying that volunteers could help in the search, but the police would be in charge.

About fifty volunteers showed up the next day. A police command post was established in the supermarket parking lot. Teams were dispatched to search the riverbanks and the railroad tracks. About forty of the volunteers were assigned to search the cornfield.

Hocking County Sheriff Jimmy Jones led the teams searching the river in johnboats. Jones was serving his first term as sheriff, having worked his way up from a job on a county road crew to deputy sheriff and then to his current elected position. Jones was a tall, amiable man, like the old Andy Griffith television character Gomer Pyle without the Southern drawl.

Jones paddled down the sluggish river in a johnboat with his deputy, Bill Groves. The river hardly merited that designation, being at this point only a few yards wide and a few feet deep. They prodded the clogs of debris and trash hung up by fallen trees and low-hanging branches. They found nothing, until they rounded a bend and the railroad trestle bridge came into sight.

Something in the water caught Jones's eye. He dislodged it with his pad-dle, thinking it was probably a dead animal, maybe a pig carcass. But as it floated away, Jones could tell he'd found a human body part; he couldn't be sure just which part, though. The object caught on a sandbar, where Jones could get close to it. He quickly realized he'd found a torso: no legs, arms, or head—just a torso. It was apparently male, though the lack of any discernable sex organs made it hard to be sure.

He radioed for other officers to come down from the riverbanks and secure the scene. As soon as they did, he and Groves proceeded downstream. Not far from the trestle, he spotted a similar object stuck in some branches near the bank. It was another torso, this one a female for sure. Jones couldn't reach it with his paddle, so other officers came to the site from the riverbank and managed to dislodge it. The second torso went floating down the river toward the railroad trestle bridge, where it stopped at a sandbar.

The daylight was almost gone. The call went out for floodlights—and two body bags. As the word of the discovery quickly spread, the volunteer searchers were called back from the cornfield to the parking lot command post. For a short time, no one could account for one of the volunteers, a man known to have a heart condition. The man was found, and the volunteers were asked to disperse.

Dale and Sarah Johnston were already in Logan, and they had started toward the trestle bridge when they heard something had been found. Police blocked them. Dale offered his help with the identification. He had once worked in a mortuary, so he'd been around corpses before. The police politely refused.

Jones came to the Johnstons to tell them what he could. He said body parts had been discovered, but he added that they might not be Todd and Annette. Another couple had been reported missing recently in Columbus; besides, the bodies were quite decomposed.

Jones asked if Annette had any identifying marks on her body. Dale said Annette had broken her leg, so her old X-rays might help identify her.

"We don't have any legs to work with," Jones had to remind him.

Sarah said Annette wore partial braces on her teeth.

"We don't have a head, either," Jones said.

Jones was joined by Logan PD Lt. Steve Mowery, who relayed Johnston's information by phone to Logan PD Det. Jim Thompson, who had assumed the role of lead investigator since the torsos had been found within the city limits. Thompson had never worked a murder case.

Mowery asked if Johnston could supply any pictures that might help make an identification of the torso. The Johnstons went home, and Dale returned an hour or two later with three pictures he'd taken of Annette when she was about twelve years old. They were the kind of pictures that in today's moral climate might have gotten the photographer arrested. They almost got Johnston executed.

The three pictures showed Annette nude. In two of them, she was holding a shotgun, with bands of ammunition crossed in the front of her chest. On the third, she was lying on a rug, her backside exposed. There was a rather cute story behind the pictures, but Dale was not asked to tell it just then. Mowery calmly accepted the pictures and thanked Dale for his cooperation. Dale never got the pictures back.

Dale asked again to be allowed to view the remains. He said his wife was distraught, and she needed to know whether it was her daughter who'd been floating in the Hocking River for the past nine days. Mowery agreed to allow Johnston to accompany him to the forensic lab in Columbus the following Monday.

The search resumed on Thursday, October 14. This time only police officers were involved. For most of the day, the searchers found nothing. In the late afternoon, they received word that someone had reported seeing a sock near the railroad tracks, not far from the access road into the cornfield. The sock was where the caller had seen it, and when Sheriff Jones inspected it, he found it contained some fleshy material. He put the sock and its contents into an evidence bag.

About seventy-five yards away from the sock, another discovery was made near the tracks. It was a plastic-coated burlap feed bag, the kind that held a hundred pounds of animal feed. Sheriff's Deputy Michael Downhour found the bag near the bottom of the railroad embankment. He showed it to Mowery, who took a quick look at it and tossed it aside. But when Jones came up to the spot a few minutes later, Downhour showed him the bag. Jones saw what he thought might be bloodstains on the bag, so he preserved it as evidence.

The discoveries encouraged the police officers to continue the search. They broke up and started walking the perimeter of the cornfield. Walking near the riverbank just inside the edge of the rows of corn, Jones noticed a spot where some of the corn stalks were broken. He saw more broken stalks, forming a rough path that led into the cornfield. He followed the path until it came to a depressed spot in the center of the field where no corn was growing. There was a small discolored spot on some weeds growing in the swale, and when he pulled back the weeds, he saw a reddish stain in the dark, sandy soil. He shouted for the others to join him, on the double.

Downhour reached the clearing and saw an area where more cornstalks had been broken, about ten or fifteen feet into the corn. When he stepped into this area, he saw five or six holes in the earth. Going into each of the holes was a silent procession of maggots.

"This has to be it," Downhour called out.

Jones came over and broke off a cornstalk. He scraped the earth away from one of the holes. His first scrape exposed buried flesh. After a few more scrapes, Jones could see that he'd found a human arm.

Jones ordered the others to call for the coroner and to go back to their trucks and get some shovels. He also told them to be careful to look for footprints or other evidence on the way. As Downhour walked back to the access road entrance where his truck was parked, he saw nothing but ordinary, nearly ripe stalks of corn.

The rest of the exhumations went quickly. The police officers simply dug where they saw the maggots going. The body parts—four arms, four legs, and two heads—were photographed as they were found and then bagged as evidence. The searchers in the field could not yet be positive they'd found the missing couple. The faces had decomposed to the point where the skin had turned black.

While the body parts were being disinterred, Det. Herman Henry, resident agent for the Ohio Bureau of Criminal Investigation, arrived at the scene. He was not impressed with the quality of police work he was witnessing. In fact, he would later say that it was perhaps the sloppiest police work he'd ever seen in his twenty years as a criminal investigator. But it was not within his charter to complain or to start issuing orders. In Ohio, the local lawman is supreme. The BCI cannot enter a local investigation on its own volition; it can only offer help when it is asked.

After just a few minutes at the scene, Henry quietly walked away. With so many officers tromping over the area, he considered it useless to try to gather evidence. In his professional opinion, the value of any evidence at the crime scene had been destroyed. But nobody asked for his professional opinion, so he just left.

By the time all the body parts had been dug up, bagged, and transferred to the back of Downhour's pickup truck, daylight was nearly gone. Jones stayed on to make one last check. He and Downhour followed the path of broken stalks, walking from the burial site back toward the river. At the end of the path, Jones spotted a depression in the soil of the riverbank. He told the deputy to mark the spot and have a cast made of it, thinking it could be a footprint that might put the killer at the scene of the crime. Two days would pass and a heavy rain would fall before the casting was made, but it did turn out to be a crucial, though severely disputed, piece of evidence.

Jones had only one more thing left to do that night. He and the coroner and two deputies drove out to the Johnstons' home on Trowbridge Road to tell them that the rest of the bodies had been found.

Dale's first reaction was to look for a way to prove it wasn't Annette. Maybe Annette's disc of birth control pills could be compared to the stage of the menstrual cycle of the dead girl. The coroner diverted the discussion to the facts at hand. The dead girl had braces, but the front pieces were missing. Could the Johnstons tell him anything about that? Yes, sadly, they could. Annette was still in the process of having her braces installed; the front pieces had not yet been put in.

Sarah sagged into a chair, as if her bones had dissolved. Now, she knew her daughter had been found, though not in one piece.

−2−

GUILTY BY POPULAR DEMAND

Shivering on the cold metal chair, Dale Johnston wished he had ignored his sensitivity to cigarette smoke. Hours ago, he'd asked for the interrogation room's lone window to be opened. Then, he'd had all his clothes on. Now he was wearing only his underwear.

It was October 21, one week after the macabre discovery in the cornfield. What had begun about twelve hours earlier as a voluntary trip to the Logan Police Department to help the investigators looking for his stepdaughter's murderer had quickly turned into an inquisition. It started right after Johnston signed a statement waiving his Miranda rights. Det. Jim Thompson hissed a question—no, an accusation—right into Johnston's face.

"Why don't you confess?" Thompson demanded. "We know you killed the kids! The people in town are scared to death. Put them at ease! Confess!"

"You're crazy! There's no way!" Johnston blurted back at his accuser.

The stars came out. The Star Chamber continued. Johnston repeatedly denied the same vile allegation Sandy Schultz had spat at him the morning after Todd and Annette disappeared. Over and over, he insisted that he had never raped Annette or masturbated in front of her. Over and over, Thompson kept insisting that he had.

Thompson decided to ramp up the discomfort factor. He demanded that Johnston give up his boots, so that Thompson could examine bloodstains he said he saw on them. Johnston complied, even though there were obviously no bloodstains on his boots. Next, Thompson demanded that Johnston take off his vest, because it probably contained fiber evidence. Then he ordered Johnston to take off his pants and then his shirt.

Johnston assumed, wrongly as it turned out, that he was under arrest for the murders. Yet, he continued to cooperate. He knew he was innocent, and he thought by answering all their questions, he'd be able to convince the police. He was wrong about that, too.

Thompson was right when he said the people of Logan were frightened. The night before Dale Johnston's prolonged interrogation, about two hundred very concerned citizens met at a youth center in Logan to talk about the case.

The talk focused on countermeasures to the atmosphere of fear. The people organized themselves into neighborhood watch groups. Some speakers said they were sleeping with baseball bats under their beds. Others said they stuck knives into their interior doorways, to better able defend against the killer who was out there. Most people already had a gun or two, but gun sales were still up by about 25 percent.

The mayor of Logan announced this year's Halloween parade would be held in daylight instead of at night, as was usual. The annual excursion to Camp Akita for the local school district's sixth graders was canceled. The wheel of the rumor mill was spinning, so much so that after one young man was questioned, he received a spate of death threats. The police were forced to issue a public statement that the young man had been in jail at the time of the murders.

Against this backdrop of hysteria, the police were under pressure to come up with a suspect fast. An arrest, not truth or even professional police work, was what the people wanted. The handiest candidate for the murder rap was the man who fit, or could be made to fit, the cliché of the "Evil Stepfather"—Dale Johnston.

The fourteen-hour interrogation of Johnston did not end in an arrest, but word would get around town fast enough. The people would know that the police knew who did it. If it took a while to build a case against him, that would be OK. If the evidence turned out to be flimsy, well, they could always make things up as they went along.

Besides the hearsay about his relationship with his stepdaughter and the rumors about the other downright immoral things that went on at the

Johnston place, Dale Johnston had one big plus as a murder suspect: He was an outsider. He lived about ten miles outside of town. He didn't go to any of Logan's churches. He didn't join any clubs. He wasn't "one of them."

Fitting in was not a high priority for Dale Johnston. There had been no shortage of sniping in the southwestern Ohio town of Xenia about how Dale and Sarah had left their first spouses and married each other. So, in 1976, Dale, then forty-six, loaded up Sarah, her daughters Annette and Michelle, then twelve and eight, respectively, his son Dale Ray, then fourteen, and his favorite Appaloosa show horse, and headed for the Hocking Hills.

The eighty-acre farm he bought outside of Logan could hardly have been more secluded. It was two miles to the nearest paved road. Most of his property was bordered by a national forest, so nosey neighbors would never be a problem. Actually, the land on the curving, gravel strip called Trowbridge Road hardly qualified as a farm. Most of the surface was rock.

For Dale, though, the place had everything he needed and wanted. There was a barn and a work corral for the horses, outbuildings where he could raise rabbits and other small animals, and a pleasant creek that provided plenty of water for the people and the animals. They used a wide spot in the creek as a private swimming hole. He bought a trailer that would be their temporary home until he finished the house he'd laid out. By 1982, he'd only gotten as far as laying part of the cement blocks for the lower parts of the walls.

Making the move meant leaving the steady work he was used to. Dale was a carpenter, proud that he could do in three days what would take most men five. His boss at the window-replacement company where he worked in Xenia kept pressing him to take on more jobs, but Dale preferred to take life at his own pace.

Still, his appearance was not that of a carefree man. He carried his six-foot frame with military stiffness, and he kept his grey hair, his thin mustache, and even his conversation all cropped short. His body was trim, and his face was close to gaunt. When the children were young, he sometimes enforced his house rules with his belt. As they grew older, he dropped the belt, but he held on to his rigid life views.

Back in Xenia, when his daughter Dora started dating a black man, he objected violently. She moved out, and Dale didn't speak to her for five years.

When Annette moved to the Schultz house in 1982, Dale padlocked her bedroom door, tried to convince her boss to fire her, and told her dentist he was going to stop paying for her braces.

He needed a free spirit to balance his harsh side, and he found that in Sarah. When he first met her in the mid-1970s, his marriage was falling apart, and she was already playing the role of the gay divorcée, though she had not yet bothered to file the papers. Dale hired her to help train his horses, and soon they became more than trail partners.

Sarah was a petite blonde with a coltish sense of adventure. She had more than a touch of brazen openness about her sexuality, and that delighted Dale. When she was out riding in the forest, she looked for a spot where she could sunbathe or swim in the buff. Indoors, she preferred not to wear clothes.

There were times, though, when Dale thought Sarah might be a bit too wild for him. Even before she separated from her first husband, she would cruise the honky-tonks in search of someone interesting to go home with. She could be charming, enticingly self-possessed, and thoroughly desirable one minute, then withdrawn and morose the next.

One day, while they were still in Xenia, Annette came to Dale and said, "I think Mommy tried to kill herself." Sarah had taken a handful of sleeping pills and had to be rushed to the hospital. She'd become depressed, partly from all the grief she was getting from old friends, relatives, and her ex about her lifestyle and her choices in men.

They were so anxious to make their new start that they moved to the place on Trowbridge Road before there was any place to sleep. While they waited for the purchase of the farm to go through and for a mobile home to be delivered, they slept in tents for five or six weeks of the summer.

One night during this extended campout, Dale was woken by some noises and left his tent to find that three teenaged boys were trying to break into his barn. He was hollering at them when Annette came up. The moonlight illuminated her bare butt, and she was carrying Dale's shotgun.

"Shoot the SOBs, Daddy!" the naked twelve-year-old shouted.

Dale was so bemused by the sight of Annette, part wood sprite and part warrior, he sought to preserve the occasion. The next day, he took a few photographs of Annette, in the nude and toting the shotgun. He didn't consider the pictures salacious or indecent, which is why these were the pictures he gave to police to help them identify Annette's body—the same pictures the police used against him as evidence he was a crazed child molester.

Dale would have objected to anyone who suggested that he and his family practiced a decadent lifestyle. He probably would have gone along with "uninhibited," though.

The heat of their spousal passion was not something they took pains to hide. Sometimes when they made love in their room, they forgot to close the door. If one of the kids came around, they usually did not feel compelled to cover up or stop what they were doing. The inside of the trailer was a clothing-optional zone, as was the swimming hole.

So, perhaps no one should have been shocked when Annette started acting out sexually as soon as she passed puberty. When Annette was about thirteen, she climbed into bed with Dale and made an awkward attempt to mimic her mother's role. Dale abruptly stopped her and gave her a stern lecture on appropriate and inappropriate touching between daughter and stepfather.

That, however, did not stop Annette from displaying her developing body during her high school years. Dale would sometimes catch her going off to school wearing a sheer blouse and no bra. He'd make her go back and change, but often as not, she would come home with her bra in her purse. Sarah threatened to sew the bras into Annette's blouses.

Upon her return from a visit to relatives in Xenia, Annette announced she was afraid she might have contracted a venereal disease. Sarah made some calls and found out that Annette had been cruising the county fair, going off with boys behind the midway. The medical fears turned out to be unfounded; Annette's problem was only a urinary tract infection.

The problem escalated when Annette was about sixteen. She tearfully told her mother that she'd been raped by her stepbrother, Dale Ray, and she was afraid she was pregnant. When Dale Ray was confronted, he admitted having sex with Annette, but in his version, Annette had seduced him. The immediate crisis passed when Annette had her period, and the parents extracted a promise from both children to keep their hands off each other. Dale Ray Johnston did not respond to attempts by the author to include his comment.

Still, Sarah warned Annette she was heading for trouble. It wasn't just that Annette was too casual about sex; Sarah disapproved even more of the type of boy that Annette was having sex with. "All righty then," Annette said, calling her mother's bluff, "make me a list of the boys I can date." Sarah did, and one of the names she included was Todd Schultz.

Before long, Todd was a regular visitor at the Johnston place. He knew Annette's reputation, but he wanted to be her boyfriend anyway. "I almost didn't date you," Todd told Annette once during a visit to the trailer. "I'd always heard you were a little whore."

Todd was turning out to be just the kind of boy Sarah wanted for Annette. He was certainly a change of pace. Todd was as considerate to Sarah as he was to Annette. He brought Sarah flowers for Mother's Day, and he gave her an enlargement of a photograph he'd taken of a wildflower.

Over the spring and early summer of 1982, Annette and Todd started to talk about getting married. They seemed oddly matched. Todd was a hometown boy and was content to remain one. He was much more interested in fixing up his LeMans than in launching himself onto a career path.

Annette, on the other hand, was determined to go places, and those places did not include Logan. At school, she was compulsive about getting high grades. Receiving a test score of 98 when she thought she should have gotten a 100 was enough to start her crying. She was a whiz at computer programming, and she was well aware that her computer skills were her ticket to a good job, a nice apartment, and sharp clothes. Among her extracurricular activities, she marched in the high school band and served as a tutor for slow learners. Her success at college level courses meant that she'd be able to enter Ohio State as a junior, after only one year at Hocking Tech.

She was also an accomplished horsewoman. For years, Annette willingly trained and groomed show horses. She was at her best, though, at the competitions. She loved wearing the breeches, the jacket, and the cute little velvet cap. And what a thrill it was to have the beautiful beast she rode prance to her commands.

Dale and Sarah were themselves an embodiment of the old axiom that opposites attract, so they did not discourage the deepening relationship between the laid-back Todd and the hard-charging Annette. Sarah started going through wedding-dress patterns for one she would sew for Annette. Dale and Todd joked about what they'd wear to the wedding—Todd going for red sneakers and Dale for cowboy boots.

By August, however, the song of love started sounding a bit off-key. Annette was training a horse to compete at the state fair. Dale was helping her, and Todd was miffed that the project was taking so much of her time.

Neither Annette nor Dale cared much for Todd's attitude. This might be the last father-daughter activity that they shared before the wedding. Dale's plan was to go up to Columbus for the fair with Annette, where they would spend one or two nights in their pickup fitted with a camper. There wouldn't be enough room in the camper for Todd—who didn't want to go anyway, but didn't want Annette to go either.

Annette didn't win a single ribbon at the show, so she came home in a snit. Then Dale tossed his ridiculous tantrum over Annette and Todd changing into their bathing suits together.

Tired of the growing tension, Annette packed some things and moved into the Schultz home in Logan. For the first few weeks, she concentrated on competing in September's Miss Parade of the Hills contest. But she didn't make it past the semifinals, another disappointment. Having young children underfoot and living in the messes they made was not exactly part of Annette's plans for an upgrade in living conditions.

When she could, Annette would stop off at Dr. Mason's office to chat with her mother. Sarah didn't like the changes she saw. The compulsively neat daughter who wouldn't think of going out in unpressed clothes was now dressing like an eighteen-year-old bag lady. Annette had also stopped wearing makeup and was neglecting her hair; before she moved, she'd frequently spent hours coloring it and feathering it.

Annette talked casually about smoking dope. In high school, Annette had been so stridently antidrugs that she gave information to police who were trying to catch local dope dealers. At that time, her cooperation had earned Annette a death threat, which had made her fearful of riding the bus to school; now, she was chatting openly about attending pot parties.

Even her love of horses seemed to be tinged with trouble. In September, as part of her activities with the Parade of the Hills Festival, Annette had been one of the outriders assigned to lead the post-parade of contestants in a harness race. She rode her beloved Appaloosa, Gatlin Sundance. The horse that Annette had purchased for $2,000 of her own money and raised from a yearling, however, was not himself. "He went berserk," Sarah recalled. It was all Annette could do to hold on to the parade flag she carried.

They managed to get Gatlin Sundance into his horse trailer for the ride home, but as soon as they reached the farm and released the horse into its pasture, it started running wildly. It ran and ran until it dropped dead. Sarah said the veterinarian found what appeared to be injection marks on the animal. She thinks the horse was killed out of jealousy by some of Annette's competitors. Still, it was part of the convergence of strange events as the summer of 1982 faded to autumn.

What really bothered Sarah, though, was that Annette was acting like she had to sneak away to visit with her. It was almost as if Annette were afraid to be seen outside her new circle of associates. What had happened to her bright and beautiful daughter?

That question was still burning a hole in Sarah's soul on Wednesday, October 20, when they held a memorial service for Annette. They couldn't have a proper funeral yet, since the police needed to hold the bodies as evidence. Sarah suffered fits of uncontrollable crying, alternating with periods of trancelike detachment. Dale was the one who was trying to keep it together, looking for things he could do to help advance the investigation.

So, when they got a call the next morning asking them to come to the Logan Police Department, they decided it would be best to go. At least there might be some purpose to the day. The police said they wanted to talk to Dale about a report he'd made a couple of days earlier. Something strange had happened when Dale and Sarah went out to a supermarket. Dale passed two young men leaving the market as he entered. One of them said hello to him, but Dale was sure he didn't know him. Dale turned around and observed the two young men. As they passed the car where Sarah was waiting, strange expressions came onto their faces, as if they'd seen a ghost. Dale's first thought was that they mistook Sarah for Annette. He took down the license plate number of the car the two drove away in, and he called the police to make a report of the incident.

It turned out that the police had little interest in Dale's report. When Dale and Sarah arrived at the city police station, the first thing that happened was that they were separated. Sarah was told that sheriff's deputies wished to talk with her, so she left and walked the two blocks to the sheriff's office.

Dale was directed to a second-floor interrogation room. Waiting for him were two police detectives he'd never met before: Herman Henry, the BCI detective, and Jim Thompson, the Logan Police Department detective who had assumed control of the investigation.

For about an hour, Henry worked with Dale, using a sketchbook to put together a likeness of the young men Dale had seen at the market. They did as much as they could, and then Dale started to leave.

"Wait a minute," said Thompson, who'd been standing silently off to the side. "I want to talk with you."

Within minutes, Johnston, after waiving his rights, was assaulted by the first barrage of what would become a twelve-hour third-degree interrogation, most of which consisted of wild accusations that he had killed Todd and Annette.

At first Dale was dazed. How could this Thompson guy keep saying that he knew Dale was the killer? He wouldn't say how he knew. He just knew.

Dale tried to remain calm. If he could just explain what he had been doing the day of the murders, he told himself, then maybe this rabid cop would cool off.

For Dale, October 4 had been just another Monday on the farm. Sarah left for work as she always did, around 8:00 A.M. Dale started his day by milking his one dairy cow and feeding the other livestock. Then he drove his pickup into Logan to gas up for the day's work of hauling hay.

He'd bought a hundred bales of hay and stored it in a friend's place near Old Man's Cave, in the Hocking Hills. His plan was to move the hay from his friend's barn to his own barn. Normally, this would be a half-day job, but Johnston's chronically bad back had been bothering him, so he figured he'd spend most of the day moving the hay. That's what happened. Johnston needed to take a brief rest after every two or three bales that he tossed into the truck bed, so it wound up taking him all day. He finished around 5:00 P.M., shortly before Sarah and Michelle drove up.

Dale remembered being around the barn when they arrived. He might have been talking to someone, but he wasn't positive who it might have been. At that time, identifying the men did not seem important to Dale; after all, Sarah backed up his story. It would be at least two years before he pressed his memory to remember who the men were. He did remember cutting short the conversation and heading to the trailer when he saw Sarah come home.

On Mondays, Dr. Mason reopened his office for night hours, so Sarah made a quick dinner for the three of them, and then she went back to work.

Nothing special happened the rest of that night. Michelle did her regular chores. Dale did a little more work before coming in. Sarah came back home around 9:00, just as she always did. The only thing out of the ordinary was that fifteen-second phone call from Sandy Schultz, but neither Dale nor Sarah had been alarmed by it at the time. A little after 10:00, they went to bed and slept well.

Thompson was particularly interested in what feed Dale used for his livestock and what kinds of feed sacks he purchased. Dale rattled off which feed he used for which animals—the chickens, the horses, the ducks, the rabbits, the sheep, and the cow. Some of it came in five-pound bags, some in fifteen-pound bags, and some in fifty-pound bags. The feed for the cow and the sheep came in hundred-pound bags made of burlap coated with plastic. Sometimes, Dale would reuse the feed bags.

As soon as the animal husbandry line was exhausted, Thompson launched into his blistering accusations that Dale had sexually abused Annette. Dale answered all the charges with denials.

Then Thompson started ordering Dale to take off his clothes, till he was down to nothing but underwear. As he did this, Thompson seemed to grow wilder, more intense. He pranced around the room with a glassy stare in his eyes. He would duck behind Dale's chair, then pop out, put his face inches from Dale's, and demand that Dale confess.

About three hours after Thompson had taken over the interrogation, Herman Henry decided he'd seen enough. Henry stayed in the room while Thompson handled the questioning, but at that point he grumbled, "I've got to go," and he left.

The break gave Dale a chance to think about Sarah. What might they be doing to her?

At the sheriff's office, Sarah had by this time figured out that she and Dale had walked into a police ambush. Sheriff's deputies kept her occupied for about two hours, asking her questions she'd already answered who knows how many times. She left to go back to the Logan Police Department to check on Dale.

When Sarah came back to the police station, the officer at the downstairs desk would only say that Dale was being questioned. Another officer tried to interrogate her, but she refused to answer any of his questions as long as he refused to tell her anything about her husband.

She'd reached her let-me-talk-to-my-lawyer moment. She called Chuck Lantz, a lawyer she knew. He advised her to write out a statement of her activities on October 4 and then leave. Lantz said he'd try to get through to Dale.

As she started to leave, Sarah heard something that made her even more nervous.

Herman Henry was coming down the stairs, muttering to no one in particular, "I can't believe what they're doing up there."

Sara didn't relish the prospect of going back alone to an empty trailer. Michelle was spending the night with a friend, and Dale Ray, who had been granted leave by his Marine unit for his stepsister's memorial service, was probably out with his friends. Still, anything was better than spending another minute in the police station.

At home, Sarah used a flashlight to find her way around the barnyard to feed the animals. She went inside, turned out all the lights, and sat alone in the dark, holding a shotgun across her lap. Later, Dale Ray came home and joined her. He took out a rifle to guard against the terrors of the night.

Back at the police station, Chuck Lantz's call was put through to Det. Thompson, not to Dale, as Lantz had requested. "Are you saying that you refuse to allow me to speak to Mr. Johnston?" Lantz asked incredulously. "I'm saying that he is being questioned," Thompson retorted, as he terminated the call.

By this time, Thompson probably realized he had pushed about as far as he could, but he went back to the interrogation room for one more crack at Johnston. At this point, he was joined by Steve Mowery, the police lieutenant to whom Johnston had given the nude pictures of Annette.

The topic quickly turned to masturbation. Mowery repeatedly insisted that Dale made a habit of masturbating in view of Annette. The more Johnston denied it, the more the police kept insisting it was true. Whatever Johnston said was black, they'd say it was white.

This kept up until about midnight. Thompson pressed Johnston to sign a consent form, giving police permission to search his trailer. Johnston figured signing the form might improve his chances of getting out of the cold interrogation room, so he signed. Soon, he was shoved into the back of a police cruiser. He'd been given his pants and shirt back, but his boots, hat and vest had been seized as evidence.

When three police cars pulled up to the Johnston trailer, Sarah was still sitting in the dark with her shotgun. But her fear turned to anger when she saw Dale being led away from the car in his stocking feet on such a cold night.

While the police executed a search warrant for the trailer, Dale and Sarah were ordered to go to the kitchen. Sarah figured, correctly, that Dale hadn't eaten since breakfast, so she warmed up some leftovers for him. One of the police officers asked for some of Dale's food.

Sarah told Dale about her call to the attorney. Dale knew nothing of the attorney's attempt to get through to him. Later, Thompson would claim that Johnston had been advised of Lantz's call but declined an offer to speak with the attorney.

It took two more hours for the police to finish their search. By this time, it was about 3:00 A.M. They left a list of the confiscated items: Sarah's shotgun, Dale Ray's rifle, some ammunition for those weapons, and some clothing.

At the end of the long, miserable day, Dale was convinced that the police would try to frame him for the murders. But what did he really have to be afraid of, other than Jim Thompson? There was no way anyone could prove he was the killer, when he knew that he had spent all of that day tossing bales of hay. He was too exhausted to be worried, so he went to sleep, thankful that he could do so in his own bed.

Dale might have had a restless night had he known that by submitting to the interrogation, he had essentially handed the police a motive for murder. Both Mowery and Thompson would testify at length about what Dale Johnston said that day. In their version, Johnston had admitted to the jealousy and sexual perversion he'd been accused of.

Thompson would later testify that Johnston admitted to disliking Todd, to being jealous of his relationship with Annette, and to touching and kissing Annette when they were both nude.

It wouldn't matter that Johnston would deny all those allegations when he had a chance to tell his story. It was only the word of a quirky outsider against that of a Logan police detective.

Thompson had made certain it would be a case of his word against the evil stepfather's. No audio or videotape recording was made of any part of the long interrogation, even though the department had all the necessary equipment. Moreover, Thompson took no notes at the time of the session.

More than a year later, Thompson wrote a fourteen-page summary of the interrogation of Dale Johnston. In that summary, there were no mentions of the issues of rape, incest, masturbation, or nudity. Yet when Thompson was called to the witness stand, he testified at length about all those things.

With no taped record, the police were free to distort Johnston's answers any way they chose. With a little embellishment, sexual openness could be made to sound like sexual abuse, maybe even incest. Add a little hearsay about rape for spice, and Johnston could be portrayed as a jealous maniac.

In Logan, a man who would sit around naked in his own home could be construed as being capable of anything, up to and including murdering and butchering his stepdaughter and her boyfriend. And if there turned out to be a dire scarcity of evidence connecting that man to the crime, some could be fabricated. And even if that resulted in a shaky case, well, he would still be convicted and sentenced to death because of his unacceptable lifestyle.

—3—

THE SUBPRIME SUSPECTS

Fixation on a single suspect can be convenient in a murder investigation. It eliminates so much of the wasted time and energy involved in exploring and eliminating alternative theories of the crime. The real investigative work can be limited to the evidence that incriminates the designated perpetrator. All other leads can simply be discarded.

Streamlining an investigation in this fashion might work if the prime suspect happens to have been the person who committed the crime.

In the case of the murders of Todd Schultz and Annette Johnston, however, the cops locked in on the wrong man. This led them to overlook, perhaps deliberately, two other men then living in the Logan area, each of whom had demonstrated himself to be quite capable of dismembering corpses. One had in fact earned the nickname "The Butcher" while in prison and then went on to practice his sadistic trade on at least two, and probably more, of his murder victims. The other was a knife-obsessed transient who fancied himself Annette's boyfriend.

The police did not want to take their investigation in the direction of these two men—but they should have.

At Madison Correctional Institution, near London, Ohio, the man nicknamed "The Butcher"—Bill Wickline—earned his title only partly because he learned to carve meat in the prison trade school. The name stuck because of his trademark method of dealing with the bodies of the people he killed.

About a month before the murders of Todd and Annette, Wickline had killed another young couple, Chris and Peggy Lerch, less than fifty miles from Logan. After fighting with Chris Lerch over a drug debt, Wickline pretended to end the quarrel, then lured Lerch up to the bathroom, where he slit his throat over the bathtub. Next, he coerced his own girlfriend, Theresa Kemp, into helping him strangle Peggy Lerch. "Hold her legs or you're next," he growled to Kemp. Later, he carved up the two bodies in the bathtub and put the parts into garbage bags, which he tossed into trash dumpsters around the Columbus area. While he was on the run after those crimes, Wickline was living in a trailer less than twenty miles from Logan.

In 1985, Wickline was convicted of the Lerch murders. While he was on death row—where he served as the unit's barber and trimmed Dale Johnston's hair several times—Wickline refused a request to be interviewed about the Logan murders. He was indicted for one other murder and was named a suspect in yet three more. In all those cases, the victims were mutilated or dismembered in some fashion.

To some investigators, Wickline was the consummate professional killer. Dismembering and disposing of the victims was an effective way to avoid prosecution. No corpse, no crime. Others, though, believed Wickline butchered his kill as part of a demonic sport.

At his trial, Theresa Kemp was asked during cross-examination whether Wickline's large collection of guns and knives might be just a sign of his fondness for sport hunting. "He did not go hunting, no," Kemp answered. "Bill hunted people."

A longtime acquaintance of Wickline's said he knew Wickline was deeply involved in the occult. Wickline told him about participating in ritual sacrifices of animals, during which Wickline offered his chest as the sacrificial altar.

Before and after the Lerch murders, Wickline supported himself primarily by heading a burglary ring that specialized in drugstores. He would then deal the stolen drugs. In early 1984—about the same time as Dale Johnston's trial—Wickline was arrested in what seems to have been an intentionally botched drugstore robbery in Nelsonville, about twenty-five miles south of Logan. Wickline also hired himself out as a killer; in at least one instance, he bartered his killing service to retire a drug debt.

The police investigating the killings of Todd and Annette certainly knew of Wickline's handiwork. On the day the torsos were found in the Hocking River, Sheriff Jimmy Jones, probably as a way to hold out some hope to the Johnstons, speculated to them that the bodies he had found might be those of Chris and Peggy Lerch.

Columbus PD Det. Jim Lanfear, who led the investigation of the Lerch case, said he believed Wickline should have been made a suspect in the Logan case as soon as the bodies were found. If for no other reason, Lanfear said, the rarity of people with the capacity to butcher human beings should have made him a suspect. It strains a cop's experience of human depravity to think that two or more such killers could have been operating in the same area at the same time.

Pixie Flowers, the woman who lived with Wickline while he was hiding out near Logan, was certainly suspicious of him. She came straight out and asked him whether he was involved. "Have you been out playing again?" Pixie said. Wickline responded with a professional critique of the killer's corpse-disposal technique. "That's what happens when you leave bodies around," he told her.

Bill Wickline wasn't born bad. By the time he'd reached high school, he hadn't even gained the status of successful small-time delinquent. He was athletically gifted and might have made an outstanding high-school wrestler, but he dropped out of sports. He started running with known drug users, but he was never caught himself. The worst offense he was charged with during his high school years was egging the principal's car. He and his accomplice not only cleaned up the mess, they waxed the car as a bonus.

After high school, Pixie Flowers began her off-and-on pattern of living with Wickline. "He was more like a flower child," she said. "He had maybe two pairs of jeans and some T-shirts, and hair down to the middle of his back."

His streak of avoiding the clutches of the justice system lasted only until he was nineteen. Over the next thirteen years, the entries on his rap sheet ranged from drugstore robberies and burglaries to pimping to running a narcotics house to murder. He essentially made the grand tour of the Ohio penal system, serving time in state prisons in Columbus, Mansfield, London, Chillicothe, and on death row in Lucasville.

"Bill liked going back to prison," Pixie recalled. In the world behind bars, Wickline could get clean from drugs and booze and pump up his six-foot-three-inch frame to bullish proportions. With his dark good looks, his thick, slick black hair, he might have made a successful pro wrestler on television.

He also took advantage of the educational offerings in prison. Besides the meat-carving course, he took some college-level psychology courses. However, he was also learning things that would help him advance as a career criminal. For example, he learned never to carry a firearm when he was doing a drugstore burglary; that way, he avoided the far more serious charges that came along with having a weapon while committing a crime. A friend of Wickline's noticed the progressive changes in him; as he spent more and more time in prison, he became more deeply involved with the hardened criminals in the prison mainstream. "Once you get in the mainstream, you don't get out," his friend said.

His advance into a life of crime was accompanied by escalating drug use. He came to favor injecting cocaine, Kemp said. The drug use would sometimes get him into debt, and killing for hire became one way of working off that debt.

Wickline's first suspected kill occurred on November 11, 1979. The body of Charles Marsh, a known drug dealer, was found in his bed in his Parkersburg, West Virginia, apartment—most of his body, that is. Marsh's killer had strangled him with a telephone cord. Afterwards, the killer severed Marsh's head, set it on a bedside night table, and combed Marsh's hair before departing.

West Virginia police investigated the case for nearly five years without making an arrest. They believe the killer had experience in cutting up large animals, since Marsh's head had been severed with only one or two cuts. Informants told them the killing was probably a killing for hire and that the hit man may have spent time in Parkersburg befriending Marsh before murdering him. Police also had information that the killer had worked in a prison slaughterhouse and was nicknamed "The Butcher."

After Wickline's arrest for the Lerch murders, police sources in that case provided the additional corroboration West Virginia police needed. Wickline was charged with the murder of Charles Marsh, though he was never prosecuted.

Three other dismemberment murders have been linked to Wickline. Tony Muncie, a fourteen-year-old Columbus boy, disappeared in October 1983. His body was found two days later, tossed beside a rural road in Delaware

County, about thirty miles north of Columbus. Muncie had been killed by stab wounds to the back. His arms had been severed, and his head and legs were partially severed. Police believe that Muncie had been an unfortunate witness to one of Wickline's other crimes, probably a drugstore burglary.

Tory Gainer, a known gambler in Central Ohio, disappeared in early 1979. Police believe that Gainer was murdered, then his body was dismembered and scattered at different landfill sites in Fairfield County. Wickline was a suspect in that case.

Columbus police learned that Wickline may have been involved in a contract killing in Florida in early 1983. They contacted Dade County police, who had an unsolved murder case whose details matched the information developed in Ohio. The torso of an unidentified man was found floating in a canal; the man's head and limbs were not found. The Florida police were looking for a killer highly skilled in carving up large animals. After coordinating with the Columbus police, they named Wickline a suspect in the murder.

Although Wickline was suspected of the Lerch murders, the case took more than two years to solve. Police identified several potential witnesses, but it proved nearly impossible to offer them a deal attractive enough to convince them to testify against Wickline. "They were terrified of him," a prosecuting attorney said.

But in November 1984, Lanfear finally tracked down Theresa Kemp, the pretty young blonde who'd been seen with Wickline. She seemed almost relieved to be found. The story she told to Lanfear, and later to a jury, helped explain how Wickline could inspire such fear.

On the night of August 13, 1982, Bill and Theresa and Chris and Peggy had a party at the Lerches' apartment. They all did cocaine and Quaaludes until about 2:00 A.M. Theresa got tired and went back by herself to the apartment she had rented under her maiden name for Wickline. At the time, Theresa was engaged to another man, but she was falling for Bill. He was a sharp dresser in those days and always a gentleman with Theresa, opening doors and lighting cigarettes for her.

Not long after she got back to Wickline's apartment, Chris Lerch knocked on the door. He was alone, he was very high, and he was wearing only a bathrobe. He wanted to come in and have a two-person party with Theresa. She let him in but avoided his sexual advances. She drove him back to his apartment, and when she went inside, she quickly saw that Peggy was wearing nothing but a loosely fastened robe.

Bill told Theresa not to get upset, and soon the four friends were happy again and headed back to Bill's place. Soon, dawn broke, and so did the party atmosphere. Bill and Chris got into an ugly argument, with Bill claiming that Chris owed him $6,000 in drug money. Chris and Peggy protested, refusing to pay that kind of money.

Bill seemed to relax, and that put Chris off his guard. Bill then pulled out a pistol and started using it to smash Chris in the head. The party had turned deadly, and Bill was in control.

He ordered Theresa to take Peggy back to her apartment and return with the money. He gave Theresa a rifle to use to guard Peggy. The women went on the errand, but Theresa tossed the rifle into the back seat of the car. Fear of Bill was more than enough to make Peggy obey.

At her apartment, Peggy grabbed up as much cash as she could find quickly and gave it to Theresa. She also started packing some clothes; as high as she was, she was determined that she was going to leave Chris after she got him out of this mess.

When the women returned to Wickline's, they found Bill passed out on the couch, and Chris was now holding the gun. Their arrival woke Bill, and he quickly disarmed Chris and resumed orchestrating the nightmare. He ordered Theresa to count the money. She did so, telling him that she had $6,000, just like he wanted. She put the money into a jar and set it on a closet shelf. Maybe this would satisfy the beast in Bill.

But Chris then made a foolish, and ultimately fatal, attempt to grab for Bill's gun. "Don't you ever do that!" Bill shouted as he started pistol-whipping Chris again. He handcuffed Chris to a chair and beat him some more. He ordered Peggy to bring him the money jar. When she couldn't find it, he beat Chris again.

Then Chris compounded his already dire predicament by starting to taunt Bill by claiming he had slept with Theresa. Still in her drug-spiked hysteria, Peggy started laughing. Theresa said it was a stupid lie, and she slapped both Chris and Peggy, trying to get them to shut up.

Chris realized he needed to end this bizarre game. "Oh, I was just kidding," he said.

Wickline was not amused. "Bill got calm. Bill got so calm," Theresa said.

Bill released Chris from the handcuffs and quietly walked upstairs. In a few minutes, he called down for Chris to come upstairs to help him fix the toilet. Chris did as he'd been told. A few minutes later, Bill came downstairs. Theresa asked about Chris.

"I took him out," Bill said.

Theresa ran up to the bathroom, where she saw Chris lying in the tub with his throat slit. She ran back downstairs, but before she could say anything, Bill told her what would happen next.

"We have to take care of Peggy. We have to," Bill said.

"Bill, I can't!" she cried.

"Now, before she wakes up!" he commanded.

Wickline strangled Peggy, while Theresa held her legs. The assistance wasn't really necessary; Peggy never woke up, so there was no struggle. Bill just wanted Theresa to know that she was now an accomplice, not just a witness.

Bill carried Peggy's body upstairs, and in a few minutes he called for Theresa to join him in the bathroom.

"Look what I've done!" he crowed, holding up Chris Lerch's severed head, like a trophy for Theresa to admire.

Bill didn't require Theresa's assistance in cutting up the bodies, but he told her that he was going to bag the body parts and scatter them in trash dumpsters. That way, no one would ever discover the bodies.

And no one ever did.

A month after the killings, Theresa married the man she'd been engaged to. She also kept up her relationship with Wickline. She didn't think she had a choice now. She was an accessory to two of his murders. More than once, she'd heard Wickline promise to kill someone who had crossed him, and now she'd seen him deliver on such a promise. She may even have kept a spot in her heart for Wickline, but as the months passed, she saw him less and less.

In January 1984, Bill phoned Theresa and told her that something might happen to him soon. He instructed her to go to his apartment when the "something" happened and collect some important things he'd stashed behind a couch. In the past, Bill had complained that whenever he went off to jail, people would break into his place and steal his stuff.

The day after that phone call, Theresa received another phone call, this one from another woman friend of Bill's. The woman told Theresa that Bill had been arrested, and now was the time for Theresa to do what Bill had asked.

These phone calls suggest that Wickline was putting himself on ice again—that is, heading off to prison to dry out. The details of his arrest strengthen that suggestion.

Wickline, the veteran drugstore burglar, was caught, seemingly by accident, in the small town of Nelsonville. A local police officer on night patrol noticed a car parked outside a drugstore. Wickline was in the car, doing nothing. When the officer looked inside the store, he saw a man stealing drugs. Both men were arrested.

True to form, Wickline quickly copped a guilty plea and went off to what he viewed as a state-run health spa. Clearly, Wickline planned his arrest and imprisonment. But why? Maybe he did it because in the next county, Dale Johnston was about to go on trial. Wickline had tucked himself back into prison so as not to be in circulation when the Logan cornfield murders flared back into the news.

Theresa visited Wickline while he was still in the county jail in Nelsonville. He gave her additional instructions. He told her to take the jewelry in his apartment and store it in his safe deposit box. She was also instructed to bury his briefcase with his important documents and then to place some other things, including the handcuffs he'd use to restrain Chris Lerch, into a storage space he had rented in advance. Bill said he'd instructed his other girlfriend to keep up the payments on the storage space. Bill also told her to make sure that his Thunderbird was kept in good condition while he was away.

Five months later, just a few months before Wickline would have walked out of prison a free man, Det. Lanfear found Theresa Kemp. After telling about the murders of Chris and Peggy Lerch, she led police to the items she had hidden for Wickline. One of the things Wickline had kept was Peggy Lerch's wedding ring.

The evidence and Theresa Kemp's testimony were major parts of the prosecution that led to the conviction of Bill Wickline for the murders. About twenty years later, he was executed.

The Logan police investigating the killings of Todd and Annette may or may not have known the name Bill Wickline, but they certainly knew of his crimes. Had they made even the slightest effort to compare the cases, they would have seen some scary similarities. But that might have taken the investigation away from Dale Johnston, so they chose not to look.

However, the Logan police definitely did know the name of a man whom they should have investigated as a suspect in the killings. In fact, a detective from a metropolitan police agency nearby gave them written notice that a young, clearly unstable man named Tex Meyers had lied about knowing Annette and had behaved in a highly suspicious manner on the night the couple was murdered. The Logan police quickly and unequivocally disregarded the tip.

In the summer of 1982, Animal Crackers was going stale. It was an exotic animal park opened as a tourist attraction about a year earlier in the Hocking Hills area near Logan. The owner-operators were a Columbus couple, Dan and Jill Wolfery. Dan had some inheritance money to invest; Jill, a former police dispatcher in Union County, north of Columbus, had previously worked with animals as a gamekeeper at the Columbus Zoo.

The plan was for tourists to come to see the Siberian tigers, African lions, jaguars, coyotes, black bears, bobcats, and other wild animals. However, in its first year of operation, Animal Crackers pulled in only about half the amount of money needed to keep the animals fed.

One person who really liked Animal Crackers was a young vagrant named Kevin "Tex" Meyers. At the time, Meyers lived in his van. Tex was a tall, burly man, who often neglected to wear the partial dental plates that were made to replace his front teeth. However, he was rarely seen without his straw cowboy hat, which he wore with the sides of the brim curled sharply upwards and the front curled down. The hat was more than a piece of clothing; it gave him his name and his image.

Not long after Animal Crackers opened, Tex started spending much of his abundant free time there. He'd often drive onto the property and pull into the garage, just to hang out with Dan Wolfery and park attendant Mike Metzger. Attendance was usually light, so the staff had time to spare for Tex. Often, Tex would bring meat scraps from his bartending job for the animals or beer to share with the other men. Dan and Mike thought Tex was a bit weird, but they'd drink his beer.

An acquaintance of Tex said the beer was probably stolen from the Hideaway, the bar where Tex worked part-time. Once the owner discovered the thefts, he had some of the regulars administer a beating to Tex and toss him out of the Hideaway permanently.

Tex wanted to become part of the Animal Crackers family, so he worked on developing a friendship with Jill Wolfery. He told Jill that when he was an infant, his mother abandoned him in a Laundromat. When he learned that Jill and Dan had only recently been married, he bought them a bottle of modestly priced champagne.

In early 1982, Jill persuaded Dan to make a place for Tex at the park. They decided he could work tending the animals and room with Metzger in the small house near the park gate.

Once he moved in, Tex started to look to Jill as a confidante and counselor. He liked to talk to her while she did laundry for the men who worked at the park. He talked about surviving in the wilderness, about how he'd applied to be a guide and animal dresser for a big-game hunting operation out West. He talked about satanic cults that operated in the Logan area and about how he knew they sacrificed animals in their rituals. He talked about his experiences as a mental patient.

He also talked a lot about his romantic conquests and failures. To Jill, it sounded sad; Tex would become infatuated with a woman and assume she shared the same feelings. He'd buy her presents, tell her he loved her, and then, after the woman finally made it clear that she wasn't interested in a real relationship, he'd shuffle on to the next woman. Once, Tex said, he told a woman whom he'd just met that he wanted to marry her. Jill advised him to move slower in the romance zone, especially when it came to buying gifts with money he didn't have for women who didn't care a thing about him.

Jill also tried to help Tex find a permanent job. She took him to her hometown of Marysville, in Union County, and arranged for him to stay at a campground operated by her relatives while he looked for work. She introduced him to some of her relatives, including her brother Bob Snyder, a Columbus Police Department detective.

Tex liked knives at least as much as he liked women, probably more. He liked sharpening his knives and demonstrating how sharp he kept them. He nearly always carried his favorite, a nine-inch hunting knife. Once, at a party at the park, Tex showed everyone what a really sharp knife can do; he took his knife out and made a shallow slice in his arm. When a jaguar died at the park, Tex quickly volunteered to skin the big cat.

He could also display a quick temper. Once, Dan made a remark that Tex didn't like. Tex jumped him, and they crashed through a porch railing before they could be separated.

In the late summer of 1982, Tex started talking about a new girlfriend, someone he'd met at the Parade of the Hills Festival. Tex seemed to be serious about her, serious enough to run up a $1,000 credit card bill, mostly on presents for her.

After Jill mentioned she was looking for a babysitter for her two-year-old daughter, Tex said his new girlfriend would be great for the job, and he made arrangements to bring her by for an interview.

Jill spent about a half hour talking to the cute little blonde that Tex brought for the job interview. After just a few minutes, though, Jill was wondering why the girl had bothered to come. She didn't seem very much interested in babysitting, and she was definitely not interested in Tex. Any time Jill mentioned Tex, the young woman looked at her strangely. It was clear to Jill that this was another of Tex's one-way romances.

Jill didn't offer the job to the blonde, and she soon forgot her name. But Tex didn't forget what he saw as a betrayal by Jill. He started acting hostile toward her, snarling at her in a way he'd never done before. One day, Jill started to drive away from Animal Crackers, and she passed Tex standing in the road with his pants pulled down, displaying his private parts to her and giving her a big, toothless grin.

She never saw Tex's supposed girlfriend again, until the newspapers printed pictures of the young woman who'd been murdered. The reluctant babysitter was Annette Johnston. About the same time Jill made the connection, Tex started acting even more strangely than his norm.

The day after the bodies were discovered in Logan, Jill received a phone call from her brother, the detective. He said he needed to talk to her and Dan, so they met the next morning at a restaurant in Lancaster. Bob Snyder told them he had become concerned after reading a profile of the killer prepared by an Ohio State University criminologist. The profile provided a general outline of the cornfield killer as someone who had a history of trouble in relationships with women, someone skilled in the use of knives, and someone who may have been a transient.

They all knew someone who fit that bill. Bob asked Jill and Dan what they knew about Tex's activities on the day Todd and Annette disappeared. Jill said Tex was supposed to have been working with a logging crew near the park that day, but he didn't show up. Tex did, however, drive onto the park at around 7:00 P.M. She was fairly sure of the time, because it was after the logging crew had quit after dusk. Snyder's cop radar was now lit up. He told Jill and Dan to talk with Tex and try to turn the conversation to the killings.

That night, Jill and Dan gave Tex a couple of beers. It was all he needed to start talking as if he were smack in the middle of the investigation. "Oh yeah, they were shot with a .22," Tex said. He also said he knew that part of Logan quite well, since his mother lived there, not far from the cornfield. Tex said he'd discussed the case with Sheriff Jones, with whom he'd worked on a county road crew a few years back. Tex seemed to enjoy providing his friends with inside dope on the big case.

The next day, Jill called her brother and told him about the conversation. It was Snyder's day off, but he used it to drive to Logan and report to Sheriff Jones. Jones listened politely but transmitted a clear though unstated message: assistance from big-city cops is not wanted or needed here. Snyder made a written report anyway.

Jill drove into Logan, intending to meet with Snyder and Jones. She assumed Jones might want to interview her in more detail. She was wrong. Snyder's brief meeting with Jones was finished, and he had already left. Jones met her in the department's public entrance area and did not invite her back to his office. She gave him some highlights of her story regarding Tex, but Jones cut her short. He said he'd known Tex for years, and there was no way Tex could be the killer. No notes were taken. No statement was requested.

When she got back to Animal Crackers, Jill saw Tex loading up his van. She went and called the sheriff's office to report that Tex was getting ready to skate. Before Tex finished getting all his gear into the van, a patrol car drove up, and two deputies got out and approached Tex.

Jill got close enough to hear the one-minute interrogation. A deputy asked if Tex owned a gun, and Tex said "No." The next question was whether he knew Annette Johnston; Tex said, "Sort of." The deputies then thanked Tex for his cooperation and left. Jill did not hear them making an appointment with Tex to come in for further questioning.

Just after the deputies drove away, Tex told Jill that he was thinking about running when he first saw the police car. He added that he was glad they didn't ask him where he was at the time of the murders because he didn't have an alibi ready.

Then Tex glowered at Jill and said, "I know who turned me in to the sheriff, and I'm going to get them for it. If I go to jail for this, I'll come out and start cutting people up." He jumped into his van and drove off, never to return.

Jill called the sheriff's office the next day to report what Tex had said. Her information was accepted with a decided lack of enthusiasm. The whole affair with Tex helped Dan and Jill make a decision about their future. Within a matter of days, they shut down Animal Crackers and moved to New Hampshire.

As for Tex Meyers, he remained in the Logan area and in the good graces of local law enforcement. When Dale Johnston's defense lawyers raised the issue of Tex Meyers as a possible suspect, Jones went to Tex and got him to swear out an affidavit, denying he knew Annette Johnston and denying he had any involvement in the murders. In the affidavit, Tex denied owning a gun, even though one of Jones's deputies found federal records documenting Tex's purchase of a .22-caliber handgun. The statement was accepted, and Tex was officially in the clear.

−4−

CARD-HOUSE ARCHITECTS

A legitimate murder investigation is a shade tree, not a telephone pole. Even when their experience and instincts lead them to a prime suspect, the people's investigators, the police, must still do the work of climbing the tree and exploring the spreading branches. Then, the case can be pruned to a straight-up-and-down theory of the crime, one that will stand up in court.

The detectives who led the investigation into the murders of Todd Schultz and Annette Johnston would have made terrible loggers. They avoided the woods, stopped at the side of the road, and took their chainsaws to a telephone pole. Before they even found the corpses, they had locked onto a prime suspect and a motive: Dale Johnston with his jealous, incestuous passion for his teenaged stepdaughter. They had made vicious accusations against Johnston, based primarily on rumors they'd heard from the dead boy's distraught mother.

Problem was, they had no evidence. They had nothing to contradict Johnston's alibi that he had been working on his farm, putting out bales of hay to feed his livestock, all through the afternoon and evening when the couple disappeared. Johnston's wife and younger stepdaughter, Sarah and Michelle, posed two additional and significant problems. They both strongly supported Dale's account of that day. Sarah and Michelle told the police that when they came home, between 5:00 and 6:00 P.M., Dale was still working on the farm. Nothing out of the ordinary happened at the Johnston household that evening, certainly not two savage murders, all three said.

The lead investigator, Logan PD Det. Jim Thompson, solved the problem by some clumsy but ultimately effective acts of investigative conjuring. In short, he pulled a murder case out of his sleeve.

Constructing the house of cards that would become the state's case against Dale Johnston started in earnest on Saturday, October 23, two days after Thompson tried and failed to force a confession from Dale.

The first thing needed was something to link their killer with his supposed victims somewhere near the time of the killings. Again, the Schultz family led Thompson to a crucial connection.

That Saturday, two sheriff's deputies, Rodney Robinson and Lanny North, were dispatched to the home of Will Kernan to interview him. Robinson was then recently retired but had been called back to assist in the case. North was a young deputy who would later succeed Jones as sheriff. When they arrived, they found Kernan had already left to go to Columbus to watch the Ohio State Buckeyes play football. The deputies' time would not be wasted.

Don Schultz saw them at his next-door neighbor's home and called out, "Hey, I've got a guy you should talk to."

When the two deputies obliged and entered the Schultz home, they were introduced to a young man named Steve Rine, who was then an environmental engineer, grade II, working for the Ohio Environmental Protection Agency. Rine was also the boyfriend of Marsha Brown, Todd Schultz's cousin. Brown was also present when the deputies came inside.

Rine began to tell the police of something he'd seen in Logan on October 4. Robinson asked the questions, and North took notes. Rine told them he was driving in Logan, not far from the Schultz house, when he saw a tall, thin man order two young people to get into a truck.

Robinson asked, "What sort of truck?"

"I didn't mean 'truck.' I meant to say 'car,'" Rine answered.

At this point, Marsha Brown interjected herself into the questioning. "No, you said 'truck,'" she corrected Rine.

Robinson then asked Rine to describe the people he'd seen. Rine said the young male was dark-haired, and the girl was blonde. The man yelled at the couple, "Where the hell have you been? I've been looking for you! Get in here!"

At that point, Rine said he did not recognize the couple, even though he'd met Todd and Annette just a couple of weeks before their deaths. He and Marsha had been eating at a local hamburger place when Todd and Annette came in and joined them at their table. Nor could Rine identify the man he'd seen as Dale Johnston. In fact, Johnston's name did not come up during that interview.

To Deputy Robinson, Rine's hazy recollection of the incident, particularly his confusion over whether the man he'd seen was driving a truck or a car, deeply discounted Rine's potential value as a witness. Robinson's assessment was confirmed a few days later during a conversation between Robinson and North. North had done some basic police work and learned that there had been a confrontation between an adult and two young people at about the time and place of the incident Rine had related. However, the young people in that incident were two runaways from a nearby group home for juvenile offenders, who were being rounded up by a member of the home's staff. As far as Robinson was concerned, Rine's statement was useless.

One cop's concerned but confused citizen can become another's star witness. Det. Jim Thompson learned about Rine's statement and quickly determined that it might be just what he needed to connect Dale Johnston to the murder victims.

Thompson had attended a seminar on the use of hypnosis in criminal investigations. He'd never conducted a hypnosis session, but he was fascinated by the topic. Maybe a good trance was all Steve Rine needed to remember things the way Thompson needed him to remember.

Less than a month after Rine's first interview, Thompson set up an appointment for Rine to come in to the police station. They agreed in advance that Rine would submit to a hypnosis session set up by Thompson. Four days later, Rine came back and was hypnotized. These two sessions yielded statements from Rine that became pivotal in convicting Johnston of the murders. Later, they would prove just as important to the effort to get Johnston released from death row. Ultimately, they would also result in a new law restricting the use of hypnosis as an instrument of criminal investigation.

The sessions were conducted by Thompson, a second local police officer, and a third officer who'd been brought in from another southern Ohio law enforcement agency because of his experience in using hypnosis. The third officer's only contribution to this interview, though, was to induce Rine into a hypnotic state. From that point on, Thompson took over the questioning, with the second officer participating sporadically.

"Was that your girlfriend's cousin you saw getting into the car?" the police asked.

"There was somebody I thought was my girlfriend's cousin getting into the car," Rine answered.

The questioner tried to help Rine along a little more, pressing the issue by asking, "Was that him getting into the car? Was that the one who disappeared?"

Rine then stated he saw "two guys" get into the car. He could only see one clearly, though. That guy had long, dirty blonde hair, but Rine couldn't see his face clearly. "It just won't come," he said.

Then the questioner tried to fill in the blanks in Rine's memory. "You got a good, clear look at the one sitting in the car, smiling and laughing."

Rine responded, "I just took a quick general look as I was passing the car."

The questioner again tried to suggest what Rine might have seen. "You said that his hair was shoulder length. Did he have any kind of facial hair?"

"He was not clean shaven," Rine answered.

The questioner tried to get Rine to put names to the blurry faces. "Do these people remind you of anyone from the Logan town or the Logan area?"

Rine's answer to that was not picked up on the tape recording of the interview. Later, though, the questioner asked a variation of the same question: "What was the most unusual thing about that? Did they look like the kind of people you wouldn't want to get into the car with?"

Switching to an attempt to get Rine to identify the vehicle, the questioner again attempted to load his questions with the answers he wanted to hear. "Were they Ohio plates?" Then, the questioner seeks to guide Rine into calling the incident an abduction: "Did it seem to you as if the girl was being forced into the car? Did you see any object being used?"

Even with all the mental handholding, Rine was unable to provide a description of the man in his memory as Dale Johnston or anyone resembling Dale Johnston. In the entire ninety-minute recording of the first hypnotic interview session, Rine provided no names at all. Rine described the man he recalled seeing as heavyset, with long, dirty-blonde hair, maybe a biker.

Just before the tape ended, the police questioner suggested to Rine that Rine will have additional memories before the next interview session.

Four days later, Thompson's hypnotic wish came true. Early in the session, Thompson tells Rine, "You communicated earlier before we started this session some of the things you recalled since the first session. You said it was probably an older male."

Rine agreed, and he was also able to identify the young man he said he'd seen being pushed into a car. Now, Rine remembered that it was Todd Schultz. Additionally, he said he now could identify the person he saw sitting in the car as Annette Johnston.

Then Thompson asked Rine for more details about the adult, setting up the request by reminding Rine that the adult was "the guy with the white hair, the older gentleman in the front seat."

Later, Thompson suggests in a question that the vehicle involved was an orange-colored, midsized car. Rine simply answers, "Yes." Now, Rine's statement could be used by the prosecution to allege that the car used by Dale Johnston to abduct Todd and Annette was the Johnstons' orange Buick Skyhawk.

Thompson posed another memory-molding question to Rine: "Did it appear to be two boyfriends fighting over a girl, or could it have been a parent saying, 'Get in the damn car!'" Additionally, Rine's earlier recollection of a man with long blondish hair in the car was morphed under hypnosis to a person with blonde hair, possibly a woman. This enabled the prosecutors to claim that it was Sarah Johnston sitting in the car, making her an implied accomplice to the "abduction" and, by logical extension, to the murders.

Years later, the Ohio Supreme Court would issue a precedent-setting ruling based on the hypnosis interviews of Steve Rine, one that would include specific rules for the use of hypnosis in any criminal investigation: (1) A prehypnotic baseline must be established—that is, the subject must be interviewed on the record before the hypnosis; (2) the hypnotist must be a neutral party, not a police officer. The hypnotist must be alone with the subject during the session, so that only the hypnotist is asking the questions; (3) no leading questions can be asked, only open-ended questions that contain no suggestion of an answer to the subject; (4) there must be a thorough debriefing after the session, to make the subject aware of what was stated during the hypnotic trance.

According to the high court, the interviews of Steve Rine by the Logan police violated every one of those four rules. That hardly mattered to the police in November of 1982, though. What they needed at that time was enough evidence to make their shaky theory of the crime hold together long enough to get a conviction. Through the hypnotic intervention of the police interrogator/coach, Rine's statement enabled the prosecution to assert that Dale Johnston had come into Logan during the late afternoon of October 4, picked up his wife Sarah and stepdaughter Michelle, then forced Todd and Annette into the orange car.

This theory implied that Sarah Johnston was deeply involved in the awful crimes. Would anyone really believe that a mother could participate in the butchery of her own daughter? The police decided to table that question for the time being. The only really important thing was getting enough evidence cards, no matter how thin, to stand up long enough to get Dale Johnston into a courtroom.

Jim Thompson was clearly the chief architect in charge of the day-to-day investigation, yet as far as the public knew, he remained in the background. Whenever official statements were made, they were handled either by Sheriff Jones or Chief Barron. Thompson stayed in the shadows, emerging mostly to take control at crucial points, such as the interrogation of Dale Johnston.

In fact, Thompson had been a somewhat shadowy figure ever since he arrived in Logan in the mid-1970s. Within a couple of years, he attained the rank of chief of police, but in 1980, something happened, and Thompson was demoted. No explanation of the action was provided by city officials. The City Council allowed him to remain on the force and even created the position of detective lieutenant specifically for him.

The council frustrated attempts by the news media to find out what had caused the demotion. Although the city turned over Thompson's personnel file, after being slapped with a freedom-of-information action by the *Columbus Dispatch,* there was nothing in the file regarding the reasons behind Thompson's demotion. A few people outside the Logan power structure knew at least part of the story, though.

In 1980, Dale Griffiths was a retired police detective in western Ohio who worked as a consultant to agencies seeking expertise on matters related to the occult. Griffiths got a call from a Logan official who asked him to come to Logan right away. He agreed to meet in Columbus with two Logan officers, who would then escort him to Logan. When the Logan officers hit their siren and flashers for the fifty-mile ride, Griffiths realized the matter was a bit more urgent than he'd originally thought.

At the Logan police station, the chief who had recently replaced Thompson took Griffiths straight to the desk that Thompson had used. On the floor beneath the desk was a small object that was definitely not issued by the city—a small cloth figure with pins stuck into it. Griffiths told the chief that the object was just what he thought it was, a voodoo doll. Griffiths was also informed, off the record, that police suspected Thompson had left it as a spooky sort of desk-warming gift for his successor.

Griffiths also learned a major factor in Thompson's demotion was that Thompson had recently made several appearances around town out of uniform—way out of uniform. Thompson had been seen at least twice wearing Rambo-style camouflage gear, with his face covered in black greasepaint. The ensemble was set off eerily by a necklace of chicken feathers.

The feather necklace was of particular interest to Griffiths. That type of ornamentation was worn by some of the cult groups that Griffiths had investigated. At this point, Griffiths was disturbed enough to ask that police officers accompany him for as long as he remained in Logan, which was only long enough to conclude Jim Thompson appeared to have more than a passing interest in the occult.

There was a cult-related case that Thompson had become very interested in, not long after he arrived in Logan. He investigated a series of animal mutilations in the surrounding area, where the carcasses of cows, dogs, chickens, and rabbits had been found in rural fields, some with their genitals cut away. In that case, Thompson and Hocking County prosecuting attorney Christopher Veidt issued a joint statement saying the mutilations appeared to be the work of a cult. However, when the mutilated bodies of Todd and Annette were discovered, law enforcement authorities quickly stated there was no cult involvement.

In 1981, Thompson called Columbus PD Det. Jim Lanfear, requesting that Lanfear meet with him to discuss a series of drugstore burglaries that had occurred in both their jurisdictions. When Lanfear arrived for the meeting, he was quickly taken aback by the woman Thompson had brought with him. Thompson had not mentioned bringing anyone. What was worse, Lanfear knew the woman was a member of The Way, an ultrafundamentalist religious sect, members of which had been involved in another case Lanfear was investigating.

The discussion of the drugstore burglaries turned out to be even more un-settling for Lanfear. The woman appeared to be running the show, at least Thompson's part of it. When Lanfear brought up the name of a possible sus-pect in the burglaries, the woman cut off any response from Thompson, offer-ing instead her view that the man Lanfear had named couldn't have been in-volved because his astrological sign ruled him out. Thompson at first seemed disappointed by the loss of an otherwise perfectly viable suspect, but he quickly deferred to the woman's investigative powers. By the time the meet-ing ended, Lanfear had concluded the whole thing had been a ruse concocted and controlled by Thompson's woman friend, apparently in an effort to find out what Lanfear might know in the case involving The Way.

Despite Thompson's penchant for the bizarre, no one in authority ever questioned his claim to the leadership of the investigation of the murders of Todd and Annette. The cornfield where the body parts were discovered was actually in West Logan, which technically should have made it the sheriff's case. Also, the prosecution's theory that the killings occurred at Johnston's trailer put it more than ten miles outside of Logan. Yet no one ever questioned Thompson's lead role in the investigation, even though he had essentially no experience with murder cases. Thompson simply grabbed command, and no one so much as raised a hand to object. During the investigation, the juris-diction problem was apparently solved when Thompson was made a special investigator for the Hocking County prosecuting attorney.

Thompson made sure that no one could question his determination. He worked sixteen-hour days on the case throughout much of 1983. He needed to. He had plenty of gossip to use as a foundation for motive, but he had no murder weapon, no witnesses to the murder or to the subsequent dismember-ments, nothing to establish the scene of the crime, and nothing to corroborate the hearsay statements of sexual improprieties within the Johnston household.

There was also the mildly troubling complication that Johnston's alibi was backed up by his wife Sarah and his other stepdaughter Michelle, the only two people known to have been with Dale on the evening of the mur-ders. The Sarah problem could be dealt with. The prosecutors would paint her as a silent partner in Dale's sexual abuse of Annette, so it wouldn't be too big a stretch to depict her as a silent witness to the murders. Michelle, how-ever, presented a bigger problem, one that Thompson would later decide to deal with harshly.

But at the early stage of the investigation, the first order of business was to find something, anything, to support the kidnap scenario that had been formed from the hypnotic haze of Steve Rine's interviews. In its final version, Rine's statement was that Dale Johnston had forced Todd and Annette into an orange car, probably Johnston's Buick Skyhawk, which already had two passengers, probably Sarah and Michelle Johnston.

Sarah's accounting for her time in the late afternoon had been confirmed by independent witnesses. She left her job at Dr. Mason's office at about 5:00 P.M., picked up Michelle at a dentist's office, bought a newspaper, and headed home. All those errands had been performed while driving the orange Buick, the flashpoint for the friction between Todd and the Johnstons and for Dale Johnston's final outburst of jealous, murderous rage.

Rine had stated Dale was driving the orange car for the kidnapping of Todd and Annette. How had Dale gotten into town, if the car had been sitting in Dr. Mason's parking lot all day? Assuming he'd driven into Logan in his pickup and switched over to the Buick, where had he left the truck?

The most convenient way to connect the dots was to place Dale at the doctor's office, where he could have driven off with Sarah and the Buick. He would have had to have come somewhere near the end of the work day, because Dr. Mason told police that his car was blocking Sarah's until the end of the daytime hours at 5:00 P.M. Patients who came to the office for appointments during the night hours told police that Sarah was at the reception desk, chatting amiably with them, mostly about their kids and hers—strange behavior for a mother who had just witnessed her daughter's murder.

Thompson's first effort to create some sort of a crack in the normality of Sarah Johnston's day was to try to smear Dr. Mason with sexual innuendo. While questioning Mason, Thompson tossed out an unsubstantiated allegation that Mason and Sarah were having an affair. Mason denied the accusation absolutely, and he called Thompson's bluff by agreeing to take a lie-detector test. The test confirmed that Mason was being truthful, and so Thompson discarded Mason as a potentially useful state witness.

Having failed to discredit the doctor, Thompson settled for Eugene McDaniels, a handyman who sometimes worked around Mason's office. McDaniels told police that he had been working on a door to the building that contained Mason's offices. The date might have been October 4, though McDaniels couldn't be sure. The handyman said he'd seen three young people having a noisy conversation inside the building. After being shown pictures of Todd and Annette, he identified them as two of the three people. The third could have been Michelle, McDaniels surmised.

This happened late in the evening, perhaps between 6:30 and 7:00 P.M., according to McDaniels, who remembered asking Sarah whether the building's lights were being kept on to aid him in his work. No, Sarah answered, it was because the doctor was holding night hours that night. McDaniels never reported seeing anyone who resembled Dale Johnston around the doctor's office.

But the handyman had said he'd seen the murder victims, and that was a big plus for Thompson. It meant that Dale Johnston must have stopped at the doctor's office after kidnapping Todd and Annette. But the young people had gotten out of the car, because McDaniels had seen them inside the building. That posed the rather perplexing question of how and why two healthy teenagers, having been forcibly kidnapped an hour or more earlier that evening, allowed themselves to be forced once again into the car by the man who would later kill them. The state never cleared that one up.

Plausibility was never the top priority of this investigation, however. The only objective was to construct enough of a possibility to send Dale Johnston to death row.

Still, there was the nagging need for evidence. The burial site was out. As predicted by the BCI detective Herman Henry, the haphazard police work at the swale in the cornfield where the limbs and heads were found had destroyed whatever evidence might have been there. The torsos provided no forensic information of value, mostly because they'd been in the river water too long. Police had learned nothing about the instrument used to dismember the victims, nor could they tell whether more than one person had participated in the grisly work. The question of the victims' missing genitals was never explored or explained.

However, one thing they did have was the impression that Sheriff Jones had spotted in the mud of the riverbank. The operating assumption was that the body parts were buried in the middle of the cornfield, and then the killer hauled the torsos through the cornfield, along the path of broken cornstalks, and tossed them into the river. In that case, the impression on the riverbank might be the killer's; the task then became to link it to Dale Johnston.

In December 1982, Sheriff Jones told the *Logan Daily News* that some important evidence in the case was being sent to the FBI for analysis. If the results confirmed what they suspected, he said, an arrest would be imminent. If not, he added, the investigation would be back to square one.

The evidence Jones referred to was a casting of what Jones had decided was a footprint, plus Dale Johnston's boots. The report of FBI footprint analyst William Bodziak was the antithesis of what Jones had been hoping for. Bodziak stated that the boots and the plaster cast of the impression definitely did not match. To make matters worse, Bodziak reported that the riverbank impression was likely made by a bare foot.

Jones decided not to share the results of the analysis with the media. He never admitted that the latter part of his prediction was the more accurate, that the investigation was going nowhere. The new year 1983 arrived, but the anticipated arrest did not.

The disappointment of the FBI report was ameliorated slightly by a suggestion Bodziak made to the Logan investigators. He said if they wanted to pursue the footprint evidence further, they might submit it to Dr. Louise Robbins, an anthropologist at the University of North Carolina at Greenville, who had gained some notoriety for her efforts to expand her scientific expertise to the field of criminal forensics. She specialized in identifying footprints, contending that the wear patterns caused by the human foot were nearly as precise as fingerprints. Bodziak offered to save the city of Logan the postage by sending their evidence to Robbins; the Logan police gratefully accepted.

At the time, Robbins was in failing health, and her reputation was fading nearly as fast. Most criminal scientists thought she was a wacko. A small cottage industry had developed to produce expert witnesses to testify for the defense, wherever Robbins had testified for the prosecution. That only seemed to make prosecutors love her more. Dozens of times, she'd provided testimony that linked suspects to crime scenes by virtue of the wear patterns of the inside of their shoes—not the more accepted method of matching footwear to shoe prints found at the scene.

It took another six months or so for Robbins to make her analysis of the evidence from the Logan cornfield. It turned out to be well worth the wait, for the prosecutors anyway.

Robbins did not attempt to match the foot impression with the outer sole of Johnston's boots, as the FBI had done. Instead, she compared the *inner* sole of Johnston's boot to the casting taken from the riverbank. She reported that she would testify that the impression in the mud had, in fact, been made by Dale Johnston. Her health would prevent her from coming to Logan to testify, but she was happy to make a videotaped presentation of her findings.

After her death, Robbins's track record was investigated by the CBS news program *48 Hours,* which found that Robbins had a track record of supplying whatever testimony the state needed to get its conviction. She certainly gave the prosecutors in the Logan case just what they so desperately needed: a way to "prove" that Dale Johnston had been in that cornfield.

There remained a few more loose ends to tie up, the most important of which was Michelle Johnston. During the spring of 1983, Michelle was brought to the Logan police station three times, and all three times she gave sworn statements saying that nothing out of the ordinary had taken place at the Johnston home on the evening of October 4.

Thompson was not ready to take Michelle's no for an answer. Shortly before Johnston was indicted, Michelle was removed from her home and placed into the foster-care system, "for her safety." Thompson then was able to call her back to the station for prolonged interrogations. He did not order the fourteen-year-old Michelle to remove her clothes, as he had done to her stepfather, but he did use the same technique of verbal bludgeoning. Over and over, Thompson insisted that Michelle was lying, that she was helping to cover up her sister's murder.

Michelle figured out a way to stop the assault. She started telling Thompson she couldn't remember anything about that evening. It wasn't quite what Thompson wanted, but he could work with it. It enabled the prosecutors to claim that Michelle's lack of memory was induced by the trauma of witnessing the murders. The defense retorted that the only trauma involving Michelle was Thompson's interrogation methods.

Inadvertently, Michelle gave Thompson a piece of information that helped him plug another important hole in the investigation. The working theory of the crime was that Todd and Annette had been shot to death at the Johnston farm, probably after an argument in the family's trailer, and later dismembered there. However, the October search of the property had yielded no evidence of such a gory crime, no evidence at all. And the rifle and shotgun confiscated from the Johnston home had been ruled out as murder weapons.

During her long interrogation, Michelle mentioned that Dale had recently enlarged a living room window, and that he sometimes dumped trash at a strip-mine pit near their farm. Thompson saw in these scraps of information a way of establishing the Johnston trailer as the murder scene. In June of 1983, Johnston was surprised to find Thompson snooping around the farm. As soon as Thompson realized he'd been spotted, he left without saying anything. Johnston watched Thompson's car drive off toward the strip-mine pit.

The next day, police returned in force, with a warrant and a front-end loader. For two days, they searched the strip-mine pit. They found some things they considered very interesting—in particular, some pieces of blanket that appeared to be spotted with blood and some pieces of paneling that looked like the paneling in Johnston's trailer. When they pulled up the rugs inside the trailer, they found a piece of old rug with spots of blood underneath.

It didn't matter that the blood on the blankets in the mine pit could not be identified as human blood, or that the pieces of paneling did not quite match the paneling in the trailer. It didn't matter that the bloodstains on the rug could not be matched to Todd or Annette, or that the small spots were nowhere near the amount that could be expected to be found where two people had been shot.

As flimsy as it was, the theory of the crime was complete. The state could now contend that Johnston had committed the murders in the trailer, and later used the renovation project as a way to hide the evidence.

The search also served the purpose of letting the people of Logan know that the terror of having such a brutal killer at large would soon end. To gain the warrant, an affidavit was filed in the county courthouse, as a public document that spelled out the investigators' suspicions. The affidavit did not name Dale Johnston as the suspect; it didn't have to. The local gossip mill had already done that quite effectively.

Dale and Sarah Johnston knew for all those months what was being said about them around Logan. Sarah had made an attempt to return to her job, but she just couldn't do it. Sitting at her desk, she would break into sobs. She retreated to the trailer on Trowbridge Road. The royalties from the strip-mine lease provided enough money for the family to get by, but the remote location of their home provided no relief from the dark cloud of suspicion. At any and all hours of the day and night, police cars cruised the gravel road in front of their trailer, crunching reminders that the Johnstons were targets.

In February, Dale Johnston went into the rumor central, downtown Logan, to the *Logan Daily News*, to have an announcement of the establishment of a scholarship at Hocking Tech to be named in honor of Annette "Tiger" Johnston. The announcement listed Annette's achievements: her near 4.0 grade point average; her nomination for inclusion in *Who's Who among American High School Students;* her membership in the National Honor Society; her ten years of participation in 4-H; her competitions for the titles of Hocking County Horse Queen, Miss Paul Bunyan Festival, Holiday at Home Queen, and Miss Parade of the Hills.

Later, Johnston took out another ad in the local paper, offering a $2,000 reward for information leading to the arrest and conviction of the murderer of Annette and Todd.

The minders of the justice system in Hocking County knew that Dale's reward money was safe. When the report from Louise Robbins arrived in late summer, the police had the last ace they needed for their house of cards. Prosecuting Attorney Chris Veidt put out the word that members of the news media interested in the Johnston-Schultz murder case might want to be around when the next Hocking County grand jury convened.

So, when the secret process began on September 27, 1983, representatives from newspapers and television stations from throughout Ohio were on assignment in Logan. For the next two days, the grand jurors heard testimony from more than fifty witnesses. They heard friends of the dead girl tell what she'd told them about the terrible things that went on inside the trailer on Trowbridge Road. They heard police officers claim that Johnston had all but confessed to those terrible things. They heard people say they'd seen Johnston carrying a gun or a knife, or both. They heard about the family strife that led to Annette's moving out of her family's home and into the Schultz home. They heard about how bitter Dale had become after her departure.

What they did not hear was all the testimony of witnesses whose information conflicted with the police theory of the crime. Prosecutors normally do not bring such testimony to a grand jury; this part of the legal process is where the state makes its case to an unbiased panel, whose members then determine whether someone should be charged with a crime. Nevertheless, police went to extraordinary lengths to make sure that only the evidence against Johnston was heard.

Ruth Cullison called police after the bodies were found and reported that she'd heard gunshots in the cornfield during the evening of October 4. A police officer came to her home and searched the backyard, since she lived near the area where Todd and Annette had last been seen. However, the officer took no notes on her information about the gunshots.

Charles Bartow, the security guard who'd heard the gunshots and was able to set the time at or about 5:45 P.M., went to the police station to report what he'd heard. An officer took a report, but police never talked to him again.

Clarence Mason, the late-shift worker who abandoned his walk on the railroad tracks when he heard strange chanting noises from the area near the railroad trestle bridge, went to the police station to make his report. The officer who took the report asked Mason if he'd be willing to submit to hypnosis. Mason agreed, but he never heard back from the police.

Janice Moyer, who'd seen the strange parade of vehicles going into the cornfield in the middle of the night, gave her information to a police officer who was canvassing her neighborhood after the bodies were discovered. He told her that the police were not interested in that; he simply showed her pictures of Todd and Annette and asked if she'd ever seen them.

Charles Blosser, the transient who said he'd seen a young couple making love on the riverbank the day Todd and Annette disappeared, gave his first statement, written in his own hand, to Det. Jim Thompson. Deputy Robbie Robinson believed this statement was worth a follow-up, because Blosser had given a description of the couple that matched Todd and Annette and had given a precise location for what he'd seen. Robinson found Blosser and made an appointment with him to go down to the spot where Blosser had seen the couple. When Robinson arrived for the meeting with Blosser, he was met by Thompson instead. Thompson told him that he'd canceled the appointment and that Blosser had recanted his earlier statement. Robinson later told a defense investigator that Thompson had several times impeded Robinson's efforts to investigate the crime, adding that Thompson repeatedly cut off all investigative avenues that did not lead to Dale Johnston.

Shirley Frazier told police a story that would have made succotash out of the accepted theory of the crime. She said she'd seen two young people confronted on the railroad tracks by an older man—not Dale Johnston— who argued with them. She'd heard gunshots and a woman's scream from the cornfield, and then she'd seen the older man emerge from the cornfield and climb back onto the tracks. She reported what she'd witnessed to police, who did nothing. Later, prosecutors would claim that Frazier had given them the wrong date, and the police also branded her an attention-seeker. Her treatment led Frazier to say later, "They made me out to be a liar, when all I did was say what I saw. I'm sorry now I ever said anything."

When Jill Wolfery and her brother, a Columbus police detective, went to police in Logan to supply what they thought was highly incriminating information regarding another potential suspect, they were curtly dismissed.

Given the prevailing demand for someone to blame for the murders, it's not likely that anything would have changed had the ignored witnesses told their stories to the grand jury. By the morning of September 29, the Logan grapevine was spreading the news that the grand jury was ready to act. The concept of innocent until proven guilty did not apply to this case, not on that day.

Sealed indictments were handed down, and two carloads of police officers were dispatched to the Johnston residence. The police took arrest warrants and a photographer from the *Logan Daily News* along for the ride. The lawmen approached the trailer with their guns drawn, but Johnston surrendered quietly. As the car with Dale Johnston pulled away, the photographer got a shot of Sarah waving good-bye to her husband.

By the time the arresting officers returned to Logan, word had spread that the killer was being brought in. A crowd of between fifty and a hundred people gathered at the courthouse, and when they saw the handcuffed Johnston being led into jail, they erupted in jeers and taunts.

That afternoon, a few days short of a year after the crime, the *Logan Daily News* printed its first special edition since V-J Day in 1945. The banner headline trumpeted: "DALE JOHNSTON INDICTED." More than two thousand copies were sold on the streets in the first three hours after the paper came off the presses. One downtown newsstand stayed open until midnight to handle copies of the special edition. That night, Johnston was moved to the jail in neighboring Pickaway County, due to the concern that he might be the target of a lynch mob.

−5−

CARNIVAL OF COURTROOM CONFABULATION

They stood in the dark in the spit-freezing cold. Better than brandy, they had the anticipation of getting heated up by the sensibility-scorching testimony they knew they'd hear inside. On the morning of Wednesday, January 11, 1984, scores of people lined up in front of the Hocking County Courthouse in downtown Logan long before the rising sun would bring its first, false promise of warmth. It was the first day of the trial of Dale Johnston.

Soon, all the rumors they'd heard and passed along would become testimony. Most, but not all, of them would get to listen to all the tawdry details of this story of sex, incest, nudity, jealousy, and murder compounded by a level of violence beyond anything they'd ever experienced or even read about in those trashy novels they weren't supposed to read, though they did. And it was all for free—if only they could get one of those precious, blank orange cards.

The cards were the passes to the allotted seventy-five seats in the spectator section of the second-floor courtroom. On this first day of the proceedings, the number of those who would get one of the passes was about equal to the number who would go home disappointed.

Some of the older women in the line brought crocheted pillows, to be used as seat cushions for the hours they would gladly spend sitting on the hard pine benches. As they passed through the metal detectors at the base of the stairway inside the courthouse, most of the spectators who were issued cards were committed to a full day on the benches. They knew they would have to surrender their passes if they left the courtroom at any recess in the proceedings, and if they didn't return to reclaim their card before the break ended, it would be given to someone else. Nobody wanted to give up that orange card.

These people had not braved the subzero wind chill simply to watch as a murder mystery was unraveled. Nearly all of them were sure they knew who did it. For them, the trial would be the necessary yet entertaining next step of the legal process that would end in Johnston's execution. For fifteen months, they had endured the fears that came with the horrible discoveries in the cornfield so close to this very courthouse. Now it was time to have their terror purged.

The hang-'em-high mentality that dominated public opinion in the community had not escaped the notice of Johnston's defense attorneys, Tom Tyack and Bob Suhr, both experienced criminal lawyers from Columbus. Weeks earlier, they had concluded they couldn't get an impartial jury trial in Hocking County, or anywhere else in Ohio, for that matter. The publicity on the case had been too widespread, the stories too lurid. Many of those stories had been illustrated with the same picture of Todd and Annette, taken before a prom date just a few months before they were murdered. In the picture, Annette was luminous with life, her hair artfully teased and carefully colored. Todd looked almost goofy with delight that this pretty girl was his date. The youth and vitality in both their faces made what happened to them even more horrible, more demanding of retribution.

So, the defense opted to have the case tried by a three-judge panel. James E. Stillwell, the chief judge for the circuit that included Hocking County, would preside. The two others on the panel were Michael J. Corrigan and Joseph E. Cirigliano, both from the Cleveland area.

With all seventy-five spectator seats occupied by the lucky and determined orange-card holders, the first session of the trial was brought to order. Before the testimony could begin, though, a vitally important issue was brought before the court. Tyack, a tall, thin man with a scholarly air and dark, thick hair, complained that prosecutors had withheld information that could be helpful to the defense. Specifically, there had been published references by police officers and prosecutors to statements from witnesses who'd reported hearing gunshots coming from the cornfield in the early evening of October 4.

Such statements, if correct, would be in direct conflict with the prosecution's bill of particulars, a part of the indictment in which the state's attorneys lay out the details of how they think the crime happened. The state's scenario held that Todd and Annette had been kidnapped by Dale Johnston in Logan and shot by him later in the Johnstons' home, ten miles away. Having people say that the killing might have occurred in the cornfield near the railroad tracks was, to say the least, inconvenient for the prosecutors.

It was understandable, then, that Prosecuting Attorney Christopher Veidt professed not to know what Tyack was talking about. By law, he would have turned over any such statements to the defense, but he said he didn't have anything like that—had never even seen anything like that. The police might have come across such statements during their investigation, he conceded, but if they did, they never gave the materials to him. If they disregarded any such witness statements, it was their job to decide what was significant and what was not, he added. "The law enforcement authorities advise me that any such information that they have checked out and satisfied that it doesn't clear this defendant, and therefore not considered exculpatory [sic]," Veidt said. In other words, if we didn't want this stuff for our case, you can't have it for yours.

In time, it would be proven that what the cops tossed out was the truth.

On that cold morning, however, there was a show that had to go on. Stillwell instructed Veidt to have the police find any statements that might be useful to the defense and cough them up forthwith. Veidt promised to comply.

The state was then ready to proceed with its case against Dale Johnston. Those spectators who were anxious for the juicy stuff would have to wait a while longer, though. Three witnesses, Don and Sandy Schultz and their neighbor Will Kernan, were called to testify about the mundane details of Todd's last day of life.

Don Schultz and Kernan both testified that Todd seemed to be very anxious to get some cash. Don said he offered to advance Todd some money, to be used to help him and Annette move into an apartment of their own.

Kernan said he advised Todd that he couldn't claim the orange Skyhawk simply because the Johnstons had promised to give it to Annette.

At this early point in the trial, the judges were mindful of the legal prohibition against hearsay testimony. The witnesses were instructed that they could testify about the general topic of the conversations and about what they said to Todd or Annette, but they could not say what Todd or Annette said to them.

During her cross-examination, Sandy Schultz testified about a seemingly minor detail that would take on added significance later. She said Todd had not consumed any alcohol before leaving the house to catch up with Annette. The prosecution would have to struggle to reconcile this statement with the findings of the autopsy—namely, that there was alcohol present in Todd's bloodstream when he died.

Nevertheless, there were some emotional points scored for the state in the testimony of Don and Sandy Schultz. The grieving parents both described their last glimpse of their son as he waved good-bye to them.

Then the tenor of the trial switched to crime scene investigation—Logan. Sheriff Jones and Police Chief Barron testified about how the investigation progressed from a missing persons' case to a double murder. They did not explain why it took the police more than a week to conduct a search of the area where the missing couple had last been seen. Possibly, they neglected the obvious because they had already locked in on Dale Johnston as their suspect, and they had no reason to believe that Johnston had ever been anywhere near the cornfield or the C&O railroad tracks.

The police had to be pressured into conducting the search by members of the public who appeared to be way ahead of them. Kathy Whalen, president of the Hocking County REACT (Radio Emergency Associated Citizens Team), testified that she and about ten other REACT members conducted the first real search of the area on October 12. One woman in the search party spotted an object in the river, looking down from the railroad trestle bridge. She thought it might be a drowned pig, but the others in her group didn't think it was worth checking out. The woman told Whalen what she'd seen, and Whalen relayed the information to Jones, who said only that he'd get back to her.

The following day's search activities were nominally under the control of local and county police, although dozens of volunteers showed up to help. Late in the afternoon, Jones testified, he discovered the torsos in the river. He also stated that he saw the possible footprint in the riverbank and ordered it marked off, even though some of the volunteer searchers had been walking in that area. From that point on, the search was strictly a police operation. Jones made another important discovery that day—the path of broken cornstalks that led into the center of the cornfield.

Sheriff's Deputy Michael Downhour was the officer who followed the trail and found the burial site. Before he left the riverbank area, though, Downhour said he saw something else that he thought might be significant. It was a four-foot-by-eight-foot burned area along the riverbank, not far from where the torsos were recovered. Downhour saw zippers, some buttons, some pieces of fabric, and cigarette butts in or near that area. He told Jones, but Jones told him to ignore it and not to bother gathering evidence.

That part of the riverbank was "just a place where the kids partied," Jones told Downhour. However, Downhour continued to think it might be important. Four different times he started to include the information about the burned spot in a formal report, and each time, Jones told him that such a report would not be necessary, Downhour testified.

Both Jones and Downhour testified that the path of broken cornstalks led only from the riverbank into the cornfield burial site. There was no evidence that anyone had made a path from the burial site outward to the spot where the entrance access road crossed the tracks, and that access road was the only place where a vehicle could come close to the cornfield. This was another glaring conflict with the prosecution's crime scenario, which asserted that Johnston had driven back to Logan to dispose of the body parts. Since the only disturbance found in the cornfield was the trail of broken stalks between the river and the burial spot in the field, how had Johnston conveyed the body parts from the access road down to the river and then back into the middle of the field?

Ohio BCI Det. Herman Henry was called by the prosecution in order to have various photos submitted as evidence, but his testimony did more harm than good to the state's case. Henry arrived shortly after the body parts were discovered to help process the scene, but he knew right away there wasn't much that he could do. "There was no scene to process," Henry testified. "There was general disarray."

He saw police officers tromping all over the burial site, destroying whatever evidence there might have been, he said. He left after staying only a few minutes. He called his superiors to report there was nothing he could do at the murder scene.

Nevertheless, Henry attempted to assist in the investigation through the months ahead. Two or three times, he said, he gave Det. Thompson written reports on leads he had followed. Henry was asked whether Thompson was receptive to the information he was trying to share or "Did he reject or ignore it?"

"Ignore it, reject it, it's a borderline case," Henry testified, meaning that either adjective would apply to Thompson's reaction.

Cause of death was not a mystery. Dr. Patrick Fardal, who performed the autopsies on Todd and Annette, testified that both had died from multiple gunshot wounds. Todd had been hit by two shots to the head, one fired from within three feet. Three other shots had hit him in the chest, arm, and back. Annette had been shot twice, once in the head and once in the neck.

Fardal said he was certain that both victims had been unclothed when they were dismembered. He was less certain about whether their clothes had been removed before they were shot. He said he found no particles of clothing in the wounds to Todd's torso, though any such particles might have been washed away during the nine days the torso was left in the river. However, he added, he might have expected to find microscopic particles in the arm wound, but he had not.

The killer had also sliced away both Todd's and Annette's external genitalia. Todd's scrotum and part of his penis had been found in a sock that was left near the access road over the railroad track embankment. Annette's private parts were never found.

Todd's torso was subjected to extra mutilation before it was tossed into the river, Fardal testified. Todd's chest had been slashed with a seventeen-inch-long cut, roughly along the bottom of the rib cage. The knife had pierced Todd's heart and cut away part of his left lung. The killer had also carved a cross into Todd's lower abdomen, about eight inches long and seven inches across. In the upper left quadrant of skin marked by the cross, there were three more incisions, each about one-quarter-inch long.

Fardal said he could not pinpoint the site of the dismemberment from the evidence given him. Both victims would have lost liters of blood from being carved up, but no large pools of blood had been found near the burial site. The passage of ten days and the rain that had fallen during that time might account for the absence of blood evidence, Fardal said.

The autopsy also revealed the presence of alcohol in Todd's blood, but not in Annette's, Fardal said. The alcohol level suggested that Todd might have drunk a beer an hour or more before his death, he said. That set up another clear conflict with the prosecution scenario, which put the time of death about four or five hours after Todd left home. Where did he get the alcohol? Certainly, Johnston had not interrupted his jealous rage in order to give Todd a beer. Veidt asked Fardal if there might be another explanation, and Fardal said the alcohol might have been the product of natural decay due to bacterial attack on the corpse. But Annette's blood showed no alcohol. It was not asked how the decay process was confined to Todd's corpse, while Annette's corpse showed no similar effects.

Fardal's testimony about the victims' food consumption prior to death presented another awkward set of facts for the prosecution. Their stomach contents indicated they'd eaten a light meal perhaps two hours before being killed—precisely what Sandy Schultz had already testified. That would have been an easy fit with the statements of all the witnesses who'd heard gunshots coming from the cornfield in the late afternoon. However, the prosecution was contending that the murders took place hours later than that, at the Johnston trailer. Veidt attempted to reconcile the facts with his theory by asking Fardal whether stress—say, the stress of being kidnapped—might have slowed the breakdown of food in their stomachs. "Yes," Fardal said, "a stressful situation can bring a halt to the digestive process."

Another autopsy finding, this one regarding Annette's fingernails, stretched the rationale of the state's case even further. Only three fingernails were left intact on Annette's fingers. The other seven had either been broken or fallen off and were never found. But under one of the remaining fingernails, Fardal found a strand of human hair that was a close match with Todd's hair. Fardal made no interpretation of this finding during his testimony, but during the prosecution's summation, Assistant Prosecuting Attorney Frederick Mong made a highly melodramatic one. After Todd was shot by Johnston, Mong theorized, Annette could have cradled the head of her dying lover and caught a hair under her fingernail, just before she herself was shot.

A more commonsensical—but far less inflammatory—explanation would have been simply that Todd and Annette had sex on the riverbank, and she ran her hands through his hair. Of course, that scenario did not implicate Dale Johnston, so the prosecution discarded it.

Next, the prosecution began to introduce its evidence of motive for the murders. Det. Jim Thompson, the lead investigator, testified about the admissions of sexual impropriety he squeezed out of Johnston during his lone, protracted interrogation of the suspect. Thompson omitted any mention of the coercive techniques he had used—removing most of Johnston's clothes, screeching about bloodstains and scars that did not exist, repeatedly telling Johnston that police knew he was the killer. In his monotone recounting of the interrogation, Thompson made it seem as though Johnston had practically volunteered the information about all the terrible things he'd done to Annette, capping off his confession of masturbating in Annette's presence by admitting that he'd done other things that were "against the Bible." Thompson apparently didn't feel the need to get into any greater detail; having the suspect say he'd violated biblical standards of behavior was plenty good enough.

On cross-examination, however, Thompson was asked to explain why he hadn't thought of turning on a video camera to record all the details, why it took him nearly a year to finally write up a report on the crucial interrogation, and why that fourteen-page report did not mention any of the incestuous admissions Johnston had supposedly made.

"This summary was prepared for another investigating agency, and all the details were not included," Thompson explained, lamely. Thompson had no answer for the question about why the Johnston interrogation had not been recorded in any fashion. He also insisted that he had seen possible bloodstains on Johnston's boots and abrasions on his hand, even though the other police officer in the room at the time, Herman Henry, testified that he had seen no such things.

. . .

Annette Farley, Annette Johnston's best friend, was called to try to bolster the case for incest. Mong tried to get her to testify about the conversation when Annette allegedly revealed some family problem. At this point, the judges were still mindful of the hearsay rule, so Farley was instructed that she could only repeat her end of the conversation. "At one point, she had a problem and we talked it over, and she did tell her mother, and—and—and things may not work out, and she wanted to go to the police. I was willing to go with her," Farley said. Whatever the problem might have been was left to the imagination of the judges.

Later, Mong tried to get Farley to reveal more about the problem. "Was any of the advice that you gave to her related to that discussion of her stepfather?" he said. Tyack objected, calling Mong's question another "attempt to come in the back door." The objection was sustained, and the best friend was excused.

Linda Anderson, a neighbor of the Johnstons, testified that Annette had shown her the nude photos that her stepfather had taken of her as an adolescent. Anderson offered no background information on why Annette would show off the pictures that would later become important evidence. Anderson also testified that she had seen Johnston carrying a pistol on numerous occasions. A few other prosecution witnesses would give similar testimony, though Anderson was the one who'd seen Johnston with handguns most often. It wouldn't matter that a half-dozen defense witnesses, most of whom had regular contact with Johnston, would testify that they'd never seen him carrying a pistol. The state did not have a murder weapon, so it was imperative that some people testify that they'd seen Johnston with something that could be construed as such a weapon.

A college classmate of Annette's, Dana Poling, testified that she had seen Annette wearing a pair of brown suede shoes on the morning of the day she disappeared. Those shoes would become the focus of one of the most bizarre, and most contemptible, allegations in the trial.

Other state witnesses testified about Johnston's actions after Annette moved out. Harold Sommers, the manager of the strip-mining operation on Johnston's land, said Dale asked him to fire Annette from her part-time job in the mine office. "He didn't want her to have any income," Sommers said, adding that Johnston wanted to cut his stepdaughter off so that she'd come back home. Sommers did not fire Annette, and the topic didn't arise again; until he shut down the operation a month or so later, Annette worked at the office and regularly went to Johnston's home for lunch, he said. A local dentist testified that Johnston came to his office to say that he would no longer be responsible for Annette's bills involving her braces. Johnston himself would later concede that he was upset when Annette moved out in the summer of 1982. He pleaded guilty to being a father angered by a teenaged daughter's ill-conceived bid for independence—not exactly earth-shattering news in the realm of father-daughter relationships. Further, the prosecution's assertion that his fury over Annette's action in August festered until it exploded into his murderous rage in October was undercut by their own witness, Harold Sommers. He testified that Annette told him that what was bothering her was the level of contentiousness in the Schultz household, not her own.

The state was under no legal burden of proof when it came to motive. Perhaps they had succeeded in convincing the judges that Johnston could be harsh, or at least in making them suspect that he was a sexual libertine. To make their murder case stand, however, the prosecutors needed some real evidence. An eyewitness to some of the savage actions would certainly advance the cause, but no one had seen anything. Well, almost no one—Steve Rine, Todd's cousin's boyfriend, had reported he'd seen *something*. It wasn't much, and his story changed radically from the time he first told it to the time he was called as a trial witness, but it was the closest thing the state had to evidence connecting Johnston to the victims on the day of their deaths.

Rine's vagueness and vacillations on the details of what he'd seen caused the first two police officers who heard his story to conclude it had no value as evidence. But with Det. Jim Thompson as his handler, Rine was hypnotically transformed into the state's star witness. Rine was primed to testify that he had seen Dale Johnston force Annette and Todd into a car on the streets of Logan on the afternoon they disappeared.

Not surprisingly, the trouble with Rine started as soon as he sat down in the witness stand. Tyack objected to the decision to allow Rine to testify, claiming that the hypnosis muddle had made it virtually impossible to "get beyond the taint of the hypnotic state at this point in time." Not a problem, the judges responded. Rine would be instructed that he could only testify about what he remembered seeing *before* his two hypnosis sessions. "Any posthypnotic statement is not admissible and will not be admissible," Presiding Judge Stillwell said.

Tyack asked that the judges listen first to a defense expert witness and then make a decision on whether to allow Rine to testify. Judge Cirigliano said the court had already decided that issue. "I think our position is this man [Rine] is a competent witness," he said.

Stillwell said he agreed with Cirigliano. "He [Rine] is here. He is available, and you can cross-examine him, as to what he said, when he said it," Stillwell said. "Am I clear out in left field?"

Tyack wisely refrained from responding to that last question. Instead, he pressed his argument for keeping Rine from testifying, but he was overruled by the third member of the panel, Judge Corrigan, who claimed that the three judges were astute enough to sort things out. "We are in a nonjury situation," Corrigan said, "and I would think a three-judge panel will be a little different situation where we will be able to separate the wheat from the chaff."

Not quite ready to give up yet, Tyack played the confabulation card. The suggestions that had been made to Rine by police—in particular, Thompson's assertion to Rine that his memory would improve between the first and second hypnosis session—were classic examples of confabulation, Tyack said. In this case, the confabulation consisted of filling in the blank spots of Rine's memory with misinformation that could be made to sound like the truth. However, the court had heard enough from Tyack on this matter. The thoroughly confabulated Mr. Rine was allowed to start telling his story.

Late in the afternoon of October 4, he testified, he stopped at the Murphy Mart convenience store to pick up an advertising circular from the racks of the free papers in the front of the store. He was shopping for a boat. He drove away and, while he was stopped at the intersection of Front and Gallagher Streets, he saw something unusual—a confrontation between an older man and two young people.

Rine said he drove off and thought nothing of the incident until ten days later when he was reading newspaper accounts of the discovery of the two dismembered bodies. "I saw the pictures; it just came back to me like a shock. Just like a cold chill ran down my spine, when I saw the pictures and I started thinking of this incident again," he stated.

He described the car that had pulled up to the two young people as "an orange, sporty" car. The driver of the car got out and yelled at the young people, "Get in this goddamn car!" he said.

As he pulled through the intersection, Rine said, he passed close enough to be able to identify the young people as Todd Schultz and Annette Johnston. The man grabbed Annette by her shoulder and shoved her into the car. There were two other persons already in the car, he said. Then, the man went around the car, raised his fist as if to strike Todd and ordered him into the car as well, Rine said. He described the man as "an older man, slightly bigger than Todd, whitish hair, dressed to the best shabbily." Rine said the angry man was the same man he later saw in the pictures in the newspaper—Dale Johnston.

Rine said he got a glimpse of the person seated in the back seat of the car. The person was a female, with a blank expression and long blonde hair. The prosecution contended this was a vague approximation of Michelle Johnston.

At the outset of a lengthy cross-examination, Rine insisted that his testimony was based on his recollection of the event before he was hypnotized by the police. "The events that I say I recalled are the events as I remember them prior to the hypnosis," Rine stated.

Why then, Tyack asked, did you neglect to tell the two sheriff's deputies who interviewed you on October 23 that the man you'd seen abducting the couple was Dale Johnston? Why did your descriptions of that man change during that interview? Why did you first describe the vehicle as a pickup truck or van, not an orange car?

"Because," Rine said, "at that time that I first talked to Lanny North, I was wanting to make only a general statement at that time. I wanted longer to think about the incident and recall back to my own memory and go back in my own mind, before I made that specific statement."

Tyack sought to impeach Rine further by using a statement Rine had made during the first hypnotic session. Tyack asked whether Rine recalled describing the angry man then as having long brown hair and a mustache.

Mong shot up and said, "Your Honor, excuse me. Excuse me, Mr. Tyack,"

"Are you objecting?" Stillwell asked Mong.

"Well, yes," Mong answered.

In that case, Stillwell said, he would overrule the objection.

But Judge Corrigan interjected and called for a session with the attorneys in the judges' chambers. During this session, the judges told Tyack that he had crossed a line by attempting to question Rine using the report on the first hypnotic session. By doing this, he had opened the door to the state's using all the posthypnotic material as well. Tyack responded that he needed to use the statements to point out that Rine's description of the kidnapper had changed radically. "If I am opening the door and permitting the opening of that statement, so be it," Tyack said.

"How can you do that?" Corrigan snapped back. He contended the court could not preserve its decision to refuse to allow Rine to testify from his posthypnotic memory while at the same time allowing Tyack to use the tapes of the hypnosis sessions to impeach the witness.

The judges ruled they could no longer attempt to segregate Rine's memory into pre- and posthypnotic compartments. They dropped all pretense of limiting Rine's testimony to what he recalled from before being hypnotized. All bets were off, and the mind games were on. "I think we are duty bound to let the state go into the thing and bring out anything that happened after hypnotism," Cirigliano said.

When Rine resumed his testimony, Stillwell explained the new ground rules to him. "Mr. Rine, you may disregard the prior instructions to limit your memory. You can testify as to whatever you remember at whatever time," he said.

Tyack returned to the taped recording of the first hypnotic session. "You were asked to verbalize the face of the grey-haired individual, were you not?"

"Yes."

"And you said you couldn't get anything, right?"

"I don't recall."

"You never told them it was Dale Johnston, did you?"

"I don't recall."

Tyack continued to press Rine on the discrepancies among his various versions of the incident. "So, when you told them (the sheriff's deputies at the first interview) you didn't remember, you were lying to them?"

"I guess you could take it that way," Rine responded. He said he gave only a "general statement" to those deputies—when he actually, in his confabulated mind, had recognized the people involved well before that interview—because he considered the Schultz home "an inappropriate place" to tell the full story. Besides, he added, he wanted more time to think.

. . .

The defense later sought to clear up the thick haze of Rine's testimony by calling Dr. Bruce Goldsmith, a Columbus psychologist who presented the court with lengthy expert credentials in the use of hypnosis. Goldsmith said hypnosis, when used correctly, can be an effective tool for memory enhancement. The relaxed state associated with hypnosis can help a person to focus, to concentrate, and perhaps to remember something in greater detail, he said. "The weak point is the suggestibility," Goldsmith said. The person under hypnosis is vulnerable to having his memory molded by any suggestions made by those conducting the session, he said.

Such memory-muddling is called "confabulation," Goldsmith said. He defined the term Tyack had used earlier as "a mixture of fact and fantasy that essentially bridges the gaps between events that we know transpired and what we think may have transpired."

In applying the concept of confabulation to the testimony of Steve Rine, Goldsmith noted that the interviewers erred significantly by failing to have Rine record his baseline memory, what he thought he'd seen, before first being hypnotized.

Another serious error occurred toward the end of the first session when one of the interviewers, probably Thompson, told Rine that he would subsequently remember more details about the incident. That obvious suggestion was an encouragement to Rine to add more to his story. The interviewer further told Rine that he would remember more about the "grey-haired man" when, at that point, Rine had not even described the man as grey-haired. Having such questions asked by Thompson, or anyone else other than the trained officer conducting the session, was "impermissible, suggestive, and very leading, and information was being implanted," Goldsmith said.

Goldsmith said the second hypnotic session was handled every bit as badly as the first. There was a "very, very high" risk that the hypnotic sessions had created false memories in Rine that later became part of his testimony, he testified.

It is not an exaggeration to say that Rine's testimony was the evidentiary foundation of the state's case. It was the only really strong piece of direct evidence against Johnston. Rine's testimony took up far longer time than that of any other witness; he was on the stand more than twice as long as Dale Johnston.

Despite the fact that the foundation was deeply cracked from the start, the three trial judges handled Rine's testimony as if they were the ones who'd been hypnotized. Before Rine started his testimony, the judges had made the puzzling ruling that Rine would be restricted to testifying from his prehypnotic memory. How Rine might be able to separate what he originally remembered from what he had been coached to remember by the police, they never said. Although Judge Corrigan had cavalierly stated that they would be able to "separate the wheat from the chaff," they junked their pretrial ruling midway through Rine's testimony and simply stopped trying to segregate the leaky compartments of Steve Rine's memory. They overlooked Rine's feeble explanation of why his story had changed so dramatically—that he only wanted to give a "general" statement to the first officers who questioned him. Even worse, they disregarded Rine's stunning admission that he had lied to those officers—that he really knew then that he'd seen Dale Johnston but he just didn't want to talk about it in the home of Todd's parents.

Rine's story only needed to hold up long enough to get what so many people in Logan wanted so desperately: a conviction of Dale Johnston. And it did that. However, it also became the key element in the appellate court's decision to throw out the verdict in 1988, though it took until 2008 for Rine's story to be fully exposed as all chaff and no wheat. Whatever and whomever Steve Rine had seen that day in Logan, it was definitely not an abduction of Todd Schultz and Annette Johnston by Dale Johnston. At the time Rine claimed he had seen the kidnapping, Dale Johnston was still tossing bales of hay at his farm, and Todd and Annette were already lying dead in the cornfield. One thing that can be said now of Rine's testimony is that by the time he left the stand, the truth had been confabulated beyond all recognition.

With Rine safely off the stand, the prosecution sought to erect the other primary evidentiary pillar of their case, the mark in the muck. On the night the body parts were discovered, Sheriff Jones had marked off a depression in the riverbank that he thought might be a shoe print. Even though any number of volunteer searchers and police officers had been walking in that area, Jones decided the print could have been made by the killer.

The casting was sent to the FBI. Jones had told reporters at that time that a crucial piece of evidence was being analyzed and that the filing of murder charges might hinge on that analysis. It must have been very disappointing to the local police when the FBI analyst Bodziak told them his best professional guess was that the impression had been made by someone who wasn't wearing shoes. In his brief testimony at the trial, Bodziak said, "At the time I examined it, I thought there may be a possibility that it represented a barefoot impression, as opposed to a footwear impression," he stated. He couldn't be more definitive, he said, because of the poor quality of the casting. It had been made by pouring plaster over the leaves and sticks that were in the depression that Jones had spotted. Also, a heavy rain had hit the area, making his analysis even more problematic, he said. "There are no real sharp features in this cast," Bodziak testified.

Had Bodziak simply returned the casting to Logan authorities with that report, perhaps there wouldn't have been a trial. Or perhaps the local police would have broadened their investigation and arrested someone else. Instead, Bodziak did what he thought might be more helpful—he forwarded the cast to Dr. Louise Robbins. Because the North Carolina anthropologist was too ill by the time of the trial to come to Logan to testify, her deposition was taken in advance, and the transcript was accepted into the trial record.

In the taped deposition, Robbins described her basic study technique, which she called an "endless method." The basic assumption was that people leave unique impressions on the ground where they walk by the shoes they wear, she said. By examining the wear patterns on the insoles and/or the bottom of the soles, she said, she could go beyond matching a piece of footwear to a shoeprint. She maintained that she could say with certainty who had actually been wearing those shoes.

The uniqueness of a person's step is partly genetic and partly the result of walking patterns established over a lifetime, she said. This combination of factors "gives us our individual nature of our feet, our foot structure, the way we walk, and the way we are," Robbins stated.

She had only published one study supporting her theories, and that had been about ten years earlier, she said. However, she had testified as a prosecution expert in footprints in many trials in more than a half-dozen states. It was only ten years later—long after Johnston's conviction and Robbins's death—that the CBS news show 48 Hours aired that exposed her testimony in at least a dozen murder cases (including Johnston's) as highly suspect and scientifically unverifiable.

At the time, however, that did not prevent her from going boldly where the FBI had feared to tread. "While the size and shape are not identical, they come so close that the heel impression of [exhibit] 24 [Johnston's confiscated left boot] fits the impression made of [exhibit] 24A [the plaster cast]," she stated. She was able to support that finding with observations of details that the FBI had apparently missed. "It appears from the depression, the rear angle at the rear heel, the length and width of the heel, the point at which the rear of the ball presses into the soil, that it—[exhibit] 24—could have made the impression," she testified.

During cross-examination, Robbins conceded that she could not tell the precise size, length, or width, of the boot that she said had made the impression. Tyack then tried to get her to explain how it wasn't the matching of the shoe to the plaster cast that was important, but the matching of the shoe wearer's pressure patterns to the patterns displayed in the cast. "So, what you are saying there, ma'am, is that by your theory, the interior portion of the shoe has pressed into the dirt, and in fact there has not been pressure on the exterior part?" he asked.

"That's correct," she answered, "on the outer side, so that it gives a clear demarcation of it."

This case was the first time in her many appearances as an expert witness, Robbins conceded, that she had made a positive identification by comparing the wear patterns of a person's footwear to a plaster cast of a foot impression. Usually, she was able to take her own tracings of the defendant's foot to establish the wear patterns, she said. Nevertheless, she insisted that she was unfailingly accurate all those other times, and this one, too.

"You were always right?" Tyack asked.

"Yes, I was," she answered.

In fact, as *48 Hours* would reveal, she wasn't—not then, not before. But that didn't matter at the time. Her testimony was accepted, and obviously believed, by the three judges.

The state used Robbins to incriminate Sarah Johnston as well as Dale. Robbins testified that the wear patterns shown on the insoles of a pair of brown suede shoes confiscated from Sarah Johnston's closet matched the wear patterns on the inside of a pair of boots worn by Annette. Two other witnesses had testified they'd seen Annette wearing brown suede shoes on the day she was killed.

The implication of Robbins's statement was so shocking that the prosecution couldn't spell it out. In his summation, Mong said it "clearly and forcibly demonstrates" that the shoes found in Sarah's closet were the shoes her daughter had worn when she died.

That would have meant—had it been even remotely close to the truth—that Sarah Johnston, after witnessing or participating in her daughter's murder and dismemberment, had snagged Annette's shoes for her own use. It didn't matter that Sarah would later testify that the shoes were hers and had only been worn by her, though Annette had essentially the same size foot and would sometimes borrow shoes from her mother. The picture had been successfully planted in the judges' minds: the mother had thrown away her daughter's corpse but hung on to her brown suede shoes.

To refute Robbins's damaging findings, the defense called Dr. Clyde Snow, the internationally recognized forensic anthropologist of Norman, Oklahoma, and former medical examiner of Cook County (Chicago), Illinois. Snow's credentials included consulting work for medical examiners throughout the United States and more than a hundred articles published in scientific journals and presented to professional societies. He had testified before the congressional committee that reopened the investigation into the assassination of President John F. Kennedy.

According to Snow, Robbins's attempt to match the wear patterns in Dale Johnston's boot to the plaster cast taken at the riverbank went "beyond the limit of forensic anthropology." That field is restricted by professional standards to "identification of skeletal remains," he testified. There are no accepted standards in the field for the kind of identification Robbins purported to make, he said.

Regarding the lone study that Robbins had published, Snow said other experts in the field did not dispute her basic conclusion that all people's footprints are biologically unique. However, he added, Robbins had never published the data that supported her contention that she was able to make identifications from wear patterns of those footprints. That contention had been challenged in the same issue of the scientific journal in which Robbins's study was published, but Robbins had never responded to the challenge in the scientific literature, he said.

Snow said Robbins had strayed from anthropology into the field of criminalistics, one in which she was totally unqualified as an expert. When asked whether Robbins's identification met any accepted standards of forensic anthropology, Snow said, "None but her own."

One of the leading forensic scientists in the country had, in effect, called the testimony of a pillar of the state's case poppycock. That, however, would have no effect on the judges hearing the case.

The other square peg that had to be forced into the round hole of the state's scenario of the crimes was the story told by the handyman, Eugene McDaniels. In his testimony, he claimed to have seen something significant somewhere between 6:30 and 7:00 P.M. as he worked on the building that included the offices of Dr. Mason, Sarah's employer. He said he stepped inside Mason's office briefly and asked Sarah, who was seated at the reception desk, why the lights were on. She explained that Mason was holding night hours, and McDaniels went back to his work on the building's exterior. But during that brief moment, McDaniels testified, he saw "three children in the hallway." They appeared to be having an animated conversation, he added.

Early in the investigation, Det. Thompson had asked McDaniels to come to the police station and showed the workman pictures of Todd and Annette. Sure enough, McDaniels was able to identify the young people in the pictures as the ones he'd seen that night. He made the same identification on the witness stand.

Unfortunately for the state, no one else who was at the office at that time had seen what McDaniels said he saw—not Sarah, not Dr. Mason, not his nurse, not the lone patient who was treated that night, not the two friends of Mason's who stopped by to chat about Ohio State basketball tickets. No one else had seen any young people in the office, certainly not Todd and Annette. And no one there, including McDaniels, had seen Dale Johnston.

The state needed McDaniels's testimony to bolster its contention that the killings had occurred later in the evening, not in the cornfield. However, the handyman's story also stretched the already implausible bill of particulars to somewhere near the point of breaking. For McDaniels to have seen at the office what he claimed meant that Dale Johnston would have had to take a break from his jealous rage to drop off his wife at her job. And while he was there, Johnston would have allowed his kidnapping victims, Todd and Annette, to slip from his control because McDaniels hadn't seen him with them. Then, even more unbelievably, Johnston would have started up again on his path to murder, somehow forcing Todd and Annette back into his vehicle for the trip out to Trowbridge Road.

The story was as thin as a poor man's soup, but it was all the state had in the way of backup for Steve Rine. McDaniels and Rine were the only two people who testified they'd seen Todd and Annette somewhere other than the railroad tracks that evening. In time, they'd both be proven totally wrong.

Two of the strongest witnesses for the defense were called to the stand by the prosecution. The first, Sarah Johnston, testified in detail about her activities on October 4, and everything she said supported the innocence of her husband.

To Sarah, the day was indistinguishable from any other Monday. She arrived at Mason's office in the morning, worked a normal day, picked up Michelle at a medical clinic in Logan, stopped at the Super Thrift store to pick up a newspaper and some snack cakes, and then drove home.

When they arrived at the farm, she testified, Dale was in the barnyard talking to two men she didn't know. Dale came inside for a quick dinner, and then, about 6:45, Sarah went back to work at Mason's office, where nothing much happened. She returned home shortly after 9:00 P.M. and, other than the ten-second phone call from Sandy Schultz, nothing unusual occurred.

The state apparently called Sarah simply to raise the issue of Dale's relationship with Annette. She certainly didn't help their case, but at least the specter of incest had been brought into the courtroom again. Sarah categorically denied that Dale had ever spoken in her presence about his having any form of sexual relationship with Annette. She acknowledged that she and Dale and Annette often went unclothed inside their home, but she testified that she never witnessed Dale behaving inappropriately with her daughter. She testified that she had consistently said the same thing in her fifteen or twenty interrogations by police. Sarah was so solid, so composed on the stand, that the defense did not bother to call her back to testify in its case.

· · ·

The state also called Annette's sister Michelle to the stand, but she could add very little to the proceedings. She testified that she had no memory of the events of the evening of October 4. She recalled being picked up by her mother at the clinic, but after that, her memory turned hazy.

There were two contradicting theories presented regarding Michelle's memory loss. The prosecution contended that Michelle had been traumatized into a form of amnesia by witnessing the murder of her sister—though there was no explanation offered by the state as to why the traumatically induced amnesia took nearly a year after the murders to set in.

Defense attorneys had an explanation for why Michelle couldn't remember any more. They contended that she developed the amnesia as a conscious, or subconscious, defense mechanism against the repeated badgering by prosecutors and police interrogators during the investigation. After her stepfather was arrested, Michelle was placed into foster care, and the tempo and frequency of the interrogations was stepped up sharply.

The latter amnesia theory was backed up by transcripts of hearings on her case in juvenile court. In those sessions, Michelle had repeatedly denied seeing Todd or Annette on the day of the murders. Nothing out of the ordinary had occurred at their home that night, she stated.

Before Michelle was excused from the stand, Judge Cirigliano asked her some key questions that had not been asked by either set of lawyers. Michelle told the court that she had never seen Dale carry any kind of knife other than a pocketknife, and she had never seen him carrying a pistol.

Michelle seemed genuinely foggy on the stand. When she testified that her memory of that evening was gone, she spoke matter-of-factly, as if she'd misplaced her car keys. Michelle was unlike her sister in many ways. She was tall and plain, while Annette was petite and cute. She was in a vocational high school, while Annette had been primed to go to the university. She was as quiet as Annette was lively.

Cirigliano wanted to make his own test of her memory. He asked her twice if she knew who killed her sister. The first time, she answered, "No," but Cirigliano asked again, just for clarity's sake.

"OK," he said. "Now, is your answer no, or that you just don't remember?"

"I just don't know," she said.

"You don't know? You don't know?"

"No," she said, with finality.

. . .

Dale Johnston's defense strategy was not to point to other specific suspects, but to contend that the investigation had been fatally flawed from the beginning, and the crimes simply could not have happened the way the prosecution claimed.

Johnston's attorneys called most of the people who'd reported hearing shots in the cornfield at the same time on that Monday evening. They called the factory worker who'd been frightened by the weird noises coming from near the trestle bridge, so frightened that he turned back from his walk to work and hopped on his motorcycle, taking the longer route. They called the police officers who testified that the leads and evidence they found that pointed away from Johnston were all ignored by the detectives leading the investigation.

Deputy Robinson's testimony, in particular, raised some serious questions. He'd made an appointment with a man who said he'd seen a young couple making love on the riverbank that evening, but Det. Thompson showed up instead, telling him that he'd taken it upon himself to cancel Robinson's interview. Why was Thompson so aggressively territorial? Was it just a case of the city cop not wanting the county cop to poke his nose into the case? Or was it another example of Thompson making it his business to eradicate any lead that didn't implicate Johnston, while he simultaneously was busy creating evidence, like Rine's statements, that would?

There was no time to sort such questions out during the trial, though. The defense was focused on attacking the prosecution's case. A half-dozen of Dale's friends, neighbors, or acquaintances testified that they'd never seen him with a pistol or a large knife.

To counter the prosecution's witnesses who had testified they had heard Annette say that her stepfather had abused her sexually, the defense brought Annette into the courtroom via videotape. Annette's taped interview during the Miss Parade of the Hills competition, in the late summer of 1982, was played for the court. In it, Annette was poised, well dressed, and polished. She was asked one of those typical beauty-pageant questions. Who had influenced her and why?

"My parents have," she responded quickly and evenly. "They let me make my own mistakes." She said her parents, meaning Sarah and Dale, would make their own values known to her, but they wouldn't impose those values on her. "My parents have helped me through a lot that way," she stated.

Prosecutors could hardly let that go unchallenged, so they called a rebuttal witness, Debra Carter, a member of the Queen Committee for the pageant. Carter testified about a conversation she had with Annette over lunch during pageant week. Carter was asked whether Annette mentioned her stepfather during that conversation. Tyack quickly objected, but was just as quickly overruled. Apparently, Annette's taped interview had opened a door that hearsay rules couldn't close.

Carter had a hard time repeating what Annette said. "She said that—she said that—she—what was she supposed to tell the judges, that her father had raped her?" Carter said. The way Annette just blurted such an awful thing left Carter "dumbfounded," she said. Carter said she asked Annette if she was kidding, and Annette said she wasn't.

Carter clearly had not known what to do with the brick that Annette had dropped into the punch bowl. Her answer to Annette's disturbing question was, "Use your judgment," she testified. She knew enough to know that neither she nor anyone else on the Queen Committee was equipped to deal with Annette's issues. "We didn't know what to say. We didn't have that kind of advice to give, and we are not qualified for anything like that. We just told her we were sorry," Carter said.

Carter admitted during cross-examination that she couldn't tell whether Annette was lying or not. It was possible Annette was trying to gain her sympathy. Annette may have sensed that she wasn't going to be named Miss Parade of the Hills and so had decided to just have a little fun and shock the committee members.

Carter, just like almost everyone else who'd claimed to have heard Annette saying similarly terrible things, was not concerned enough to act. She didn't report the crime or even tell the supposed victim to report it. She had just said sorry.

As the trial passed the three-week mark and approached its conclusion, the time came for the event most anticipated by the people who had stood in line for hours in the predawn darkness and cold. Dale Johnston took the stand.

Anyone who'd been counting on an emotional denouement, however, was disappointed. Throughout his nearly two hours on the stand, Johnston maintained the stoic, standoffish persona that had allowed the prosecution to fit him so easily into their evil-stepfather scenario.

When he spoke of taking the nude photos of twelve-year-old Annette on the day after she'd run out of the tent naked and armed to help him chase off the burglars, he did so without a trace of embarrassment. He hadn't seen it as the least bit inappropriate, so why should anyone else?

When he testified about turning those same photos over to police, he sounded like a concerned citizen seeking only to help law enforcement. It didn't seem to register, either back then or as he was testifying, that he was giving the authorities a loaded gun that they would eagerly turn on him.

When he cited his funeral-home training to support his offer to view his stepdaughter's butchered remains, it didn't seem to occur to him that police might find that a strange reaction from a close relative of the victim.

On the stand, Johnston exhibited the same why-am-I-here demeanor that he had exhibited during the long interrogation by Thompson. He had chosen to take the stand, just as he had chosen to endure the interrogation for hours longer than he was legally required to do so. To some, it might have looked as if Johnston thought he was better and smarter than the small-town dimwits who had all been so ready to believe the worst of him. Or maybe he knew he was innocent and he simply couldn't understand why the others refused to believe him.

Tyack guided Johnston through a nearly nostalgic-sounding history of his family life with Sarah. They were both in failing marriages when they met in Xenia, a small city in southern Ohio. Not long after they divorced their spouses and married each other, they took their blended family to Hocking County, thinking incorrectly that they were getting away from small-town gossips.

A complication in the completion of their purchase of the farm on Trowbridge Road meant that they couldn't move a trailer onto their property for a few weeks after they arrived. That was why they were sleeping in tents on the night when Annette routed the prowlers. Johnston said the pictures he took of her the next day were meant simply to be an innocent memorial of the event.

"We gave her our word that no one would ever see those pictures, that some time later or when she had children of her own, we would give the pictures to her, so she could tell her kids how rough it was when she was a youngster," he said. He could not know at the time that the promise would be broken as a result of the murders. Annette's body would be violated, and after that so would her privacy. Johnston gave the pictures to the police, the police confiscated them as evidence, and they became part of the permanent record of the case.

Johnston testified that there was one occasion of contact between him and Annette that might be considered inappropriate, but his defense attorney told him not to get into any specific details. Other than that, he insisted, there had been no sexual improprieties, no touching, no masturbating in her presence, and certainly no rape.

Within a few months of the first time Annette brought Todd to their home, in February 1982, the young couple was already talking about marriage. Johnston said he asked them only to wait until Annette had graduated from college, and they agreed.

Cars were a source of friction between Johnston and Todd, even before what the prosecution called the ultimately fatal fight over the orange Skyhawk. After Todd wrecked the car he was driving, Johnston sold him a drivable clunker for $400. Todd made a few small payments, but stopped when he suffered the hernia injury at the print shop. After he recovered, Todd never resumed the payments, Johnston said. Somehow, though, Todd was finding money to travel and to buy things like "fireworks and dishes," Johnston said. So, he took Todd to small claims court and won.

With regard to the orange Skyhawk, Johnston said there was never any fighting over it in his household. Annette knew it was her graduation gift, but she never objected to Sarah using it temporarily. Royalties from the strip-mining operation would come to the Johnstons in a few weeks, and then Sarah would get a reliable car, and Annette would get the Skyhawk. It wasn't even a topic of conversation, much less a motive for murder.

The closest Johnston came to displaying any emotions was when he testified about the love for horses that he and Annette shared. He was clearly proud when he spoke of her devotion to the animals and her many accomplishments as a horsewoman.

"You loved that little girl, didn't you?" Tyack asked him.

"Yes I did," Johnston answered firmly.

The state fair horse show, the last horse event Johnston and Annette attended, was also the source of a tiff with Todd. Todd wanted to come along, but Dale told him there wasn't room for three in the camper. Dale suggested that Todd drive up to the fair early on the morning when Annette was showing her horse so that he could help her. Todd didn't care for that plan, and he didn't come to the fair.

Not long after the trip to the fair in Columbus, Johnston confronted Todd and Annette angrily when he found them changing clothes in the same room. Todd left, and that was the last time Johnston ever saw him. Annette stayed long enough to berate Johnston for what she thought was hypocritical behavior; after all, if it was OK for her to be naked in front of them, why couldn't she change into a bathing suit with Todd? Dale responded with a timeworn parental ultimatum: If Annette didn't like the house rules, she could leave. The next day, Annette called his bluff and moved out, without telling either him or Sarah.

Johnston conceded he got angry when Annette left. He padlocked her bedroom door, tried to get her fired from her part-time job, and put her dentist on notice that he was no longer responsible for her bills. But things cooled down after a few days. Annette apologized for her huffy departure, and soon she started coming to the trailer from the strip-mine office to have lunch with him.

"She told me one of the reasons she moved out was to get her head on straight," Johnston testified. "Before she made a commitment to live with Todd the rest of her life, she wanted to be sure they was [sic] compatible."

In late September, Dale and Sarah went on a week's vacation to North Carolina. While they were gone, Annette came out to the trailer to spend the nights with Michelle. Sarah came down with a toothache, and they cut their trip short. They returned home late on the night of Wednesday, September 30. Annette woke up and joined them in a family chat that lasted until perhaps 4:00 A.M., he said. "She was her normal, bouncy self," Johnston said. When Annette left the next morning, it was the last time he saw her alive.

The following Monday, October 4, was just another day of work for him. He said he drove into town in the morning to gas up his truck. Then he went to a friend's barn where he'd stored some hay he had purchased, loaded up

Annette Cooper Johnston. (High School Yearbook photo, 1982)

Todd Schultz. (High School Yearbook photo, 1981)

Todd and Annette at her high school graduation, May 1982. (Courtesy Dale N. Johnston)

Annette at her high school graduation, May 1982. (Courtesy Dale N. Johnston)

C&O Railway trestle bridge over the Hocking River, where Todd and Annette walked from Logan to West Logan about an hour before their murder. (Photo by Bill Osinski)

Dale and Sarah Johnston, October 1982, in search staging area in Logan, after receiving news that body parts had been found in the Hocking River. (*Associated Press* photo)

Hocking County sheriff's deputy Mike Downhour searching cornfield with a metal detector a few days after Todd's and Annette's body parts were discovered buried in the field. (*Columbus Dispatch* photo)

The cornfield where victims were shot and body parts buried. The Hocking River is beyond the tree line. (Photo by Bill Osinski)

Sarah Johnston bidding good-bye to Dale Johnston, seated in police cruiser, after his arrest at their home September, 1983. Hocking County sheriff Jimmy Jones stands behind her. (*Columbus Dispatch* photo)

Sarah Johnston overcome with emotion during an interview, October 1984. (*Columbus Dispatch* photo)

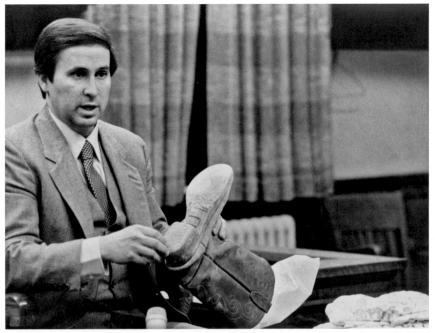

William Bodziak, FBI footprint expert, testifying at trial of Dale Johnston, January 1984. He testified he could not match a print found on the riverbank to Johnston's boot, which he is holding. Bodziak stated the print was likely that of a bare foot. (*Logan Daily News* photo)

Bench conference during trial of Dale N. Johnston, January 1984. The members of the three-judge panel, shown facing the camera, are James E. Stillwell (left), Michael J. Corrigan (center), and Joseph E. Cirigliano (right). (*Logan Daily News* photo)

Dale Johnston, conferring with his defense attorney, Robert Suhr, during civil trial of Johnston's suit for wrongful imprisonment, 1992. Suhr also represented Johnston at the 1984 murder trial. (*Columbus Dispatch* photo)

Sandra Schultz, mother of Todd Schultz, holds the hand of her daughter Kendra, moments before verdict is announced at the trial of Dale Johnston. (*Logan Daily News* photo)

Crowd in hall of the Hocking County courthouse, cheering the announcement of the guilty verdict against Dale Johnston, January 1984. (*Columbus Dispatch* photo)

Frederick Mong, prosecuting attorney, being interviewed by the author after the conviction of Dale Johnston. (*Logan Daily News* photo)

Above: Dale Johnston being led out of the Hocking County Jail by Sheriff Jimmy Jones, after Johnston's indictment, September 1983. Deputy Lannie North (now the sheriff) is behind Johnston, who was being moved to an undisclosed jail for reasons of safety. (*Columbus Dispatch* photo)

Right: Dale Johnston being led away from the Hocking County courthouse, after being sentenced to death, March 1984. The two deputies are Lannie North (left) and Bert Clay (right). (*Columbus Dispatch* photo)

Dale Johnston, shown in front of a map of the crime scene, in defense attorney Bob Suhr's office in Columbus after Johnston's civil suit for wrongful imprisonment, December 1992. (*Columbus Dispatch* photo)

Kenneth (Kenny) Linscott, in handcuffs, after his September 2008 arrest for the murders of Todd Schultz and Annette Cooper Johnston. Hocking County sheriff's deputy Matt Speckman walks ahead of Linscott. (*Logan Daily News* photo)

Kenny Linscott (right, in inmate clothes) during his arraignment on murder charges, September 2008. (*Columbus Dispatch* photo)

Chester McKnight, seated second from left, slumps in his chair during the arraignment, September 2008. (*Columbus Dispatch* photo)

Kenny Linscott during arraignment.
(*Columbus Dispatch* photo)

Chester McKnight during arraignment.
(*Columbus Dispatch* photo)

Chester McKnight (standing) during arraignment. (*Columbus Dispatch* photo)

Chester McKnight at Madison Correctional Institution, London, Ohio, 2009. (Photo by Bill Osinski)

The Hocking River near downtown Logan. The rock outcropping downstream from this point was the site of the dismemberments. (Photo by Bill Osinski)

Above: A closer view of the rock outcropping in the Hocking River. (Photo by Bill Osinski)

Left: Judy Linscott shown at her home near Logan in 2010. About 25 years after the murders, she told investigators where Todd and Annette went after they walked the railroad tracks into West Logan on the day they were killed. (Photo by Bill Osinski)

Left: Rodney Robinson (seated) and Jim Powers (standing) shown at Powers's home in Hocking County, 2010. Their persistence in pursuing the truth after Johnston's conviction led to the reopening of the case. (Photo by Bill Osinski)

Below: Sarah Johnston Brown at her home in Southeastern Ohio, 2010. (Photo by Bill Osinski)

Dale Johnston shown at his home in Central Ohio, 2009. (Photo by Bill Osinski)

Dale Johnston, 2009. (Photo by Bill Osinski)

about fifty bales, and scattered the hay around his farm for his livestock. After a lunch break, he went back to the barn, loaded fifty more bales, brought them back to his farm, and put them into his barn. It was early evening by the time he was finished.

He was in his barnyard talking to two men when Sarah and Michelle pulled up to the trailer. He couldn't be sure who the men were. Since it was such an unremarkable day, he never imagined that he might need them to corroborate his alibi in a murder case. As he prepared to go to trial, he still didn't think it was important to try to identify them. He mistakenly, and naively, believed his innocence would be obvious to the court.

Johnston went to the trailer and had a cup of coffee and a light meal with Sarah and Michelle. Sarah went back to Dr. Mason's office, Michelle went outside to do her chores, and Johnston settled in to read the newspaper Sarah had brought home. Sarah came home some time after 9:00 P.M., and they went to bed early. The only thing of note that happened that night was the curt phone call from Sandy Schultz.

The next morning started out to be just as ordinary as the day before. Johnston fed his animals, but the work was interrupted by a phone call from Sarah. She was highly upset; Sandy Schultz had just called her at work to tell her Todd and Annette were missing. Johnston drove into Logan, and his life would never be ordinary again.

In testifying about the day he first knew he was a suspect, Johnston gave an account of his single police interrogation that differed drastically from that of his interrogator, Jim Thompson. First, he absolutely denied making any admissions of sexual improprieties with Annette, as Thompson had testified. Johnston also claimed that Lt. Steve Mowery was lying when he testified that he had heard those admissions. Mowery only spent a few moments in the room, and nothing about sexual contacts with Annette was discussed during that time, Johnston said. Thompson had made repeated accusations about what he was supposed to have done to Annette, and Johnston said he denied them each time. Thompson just kept on shouting the same charges at him, he said.

"He was just constantly prancing around the room, accusing me of having sex with Annette, having killed Annette," Johnston said. Johnston said he agreed to submit to a lie-detector test. The police never approached Johnston again about taking such a test, though it is highly unlikely his attorneys would have allowed him to take any test administered by Logan police. His offer also did nothing to change Thompson's interrogation tactics, he said. "He went right back to prancing around the room, accusing me of all sorts of things, and this just went on and on and on and on," he said.

Thompson's tendency to substitute accusations for evidence continued right on through the trial, but for this trial, it would be enough.

At the close of Johnston's direct examination, his attorneys asked him all the core questions, and Johnston gave the same one-word answer to each. No, he never saw Todd and Annette that day. No, he didn't kill them. No, he didn't cut up their bodies. No, he didn't bury their limbs and heads in the cornfield.

Then, finally, the man charged with committing the most horrible murders in the history of Hocking County was ready to face his accusers, the people's attorneys. Surely, this would be the ultimate showdown of the trial, the one envisioned by all the people who'd spent all those hours waiting in the cold. The prosecutors would finally get their shot at Johnston on the witness stand, where they could tee off on him, tear his denials to shreds, and expose all his lies.

They whiffed. Mong's cross-examination of Johnston turned out to be more like an inventory exercise at Walmart than a Perry Mason–style confrontation where the guilty party breaks down and confesses. In a steady, matter-of-fact tone, Mong walked Johnston through many of the ultimately irrelevant details of the case. The bulk of the questions were about living arrangements at the Johnston household, about the various car deals mentioned in earlier testimony, about the nude pictures of Annette, about Johnston's actions in response to her leaving home, about his relationships with some of the people who had testified against him. Mong never treated Johnston with hostility, never tried to trap him in a lie, and never challenged any of Johnston's answers.

Mong stayed away from any questions about Johnston's alleged jealousy over Annette's relationship with Todd. He asked nothing about the allegations he had raped his stepdaughter. He never explored the area of Johnston's feelings toward Todd or about Todd's plans to take away the stepdaughter that Johnston was supposedly fixated on. He even avoided walking through the door opened by the defense when Johnston had admitted one possible instance of impropriety with Annette. He never asked when it happened, what happened, or whether it ever happened again. He simply never bothered to inquire.

He never demanded that Johnston deny under oath that he had made the footprint that became the crucial piece of state's evidence. He never grilled Johnston regarding the abduction about which Steve Rine had testified in such great length.

All in all, it was a rather polite half hour. The defendant was excused.

A Saturday session was called for the next day, January 28. That was a sure sign the judges expected to be able to wrap things up before the weekend was out.

Before going into open court, Stillwell made a startling announcement to the defense attorneys. He told them that about twenty letters containing death threats against the judges had been received during the trial. He offered to let the defense attorneys examine the letters, but at this point Tyack and Suhr were confident that they'd successfully attacked the state's case and that they would receive an impartial verdict from the three judges. So, they declined Stillwell's offer—a decision they would later regret.

After a few brief rebuttal witnesses, the prosecution began its final summation of its case. Mong started his closing argument in the same nonargumentative manner he'd displayed throughout the trial. He rehashed the details of the day of the murders, the movements of the victims and the members of the Johnston family.

Then he started to tie together the loose ends of the testimony of the prosecution's witnesses. He expanded on some of McDaniels's testimony about the phantom stopover at Dr. Mason's office after the phantom abduction. He even invented a theme for the animated discussion that McDaniels had claimed to have glimpsed, but not heard. The fight that led to the killings, Mong declared, was all about the little orange Skyhawk.

"And so the anger and argument and ultimate issue was to be settled," Mong stated. "He [Todd] knew he couldn't do anything through legal means, so it must be settled, and out to Trowbridge Road to settle this argument." Mong was actually asking the judges to believe that a nineteen-year-old man, who'd been abducted with his fiancée an hour or so earlier, would willingly go with his abductor to his abductor's home so that he could press his claim for a used car.

Mong next asked the judges to believe that Michelle Johnston, who before being browbeaten by police interrogators had consistently stated that nothing unusual had happened that day, had actually witnessed the murders. "What traumatic event did her eyes behold that would cause psychogenic amnesia?" Mong asked rhetorically.

The judges were also invited by Mong, a former Protestant minister, to imagine the death scene worthy of a Savonarola. Mong invoked the image of Annette cradling the head of her dying lover, who'd just been shot by her maniacally jealous stepfather. "Grabbing his head in a fashion with such intensity the hair on his head stuck under her fingernails," Mong gushed.

Since there was no evidence of any such bloody crimes found in the Johnston's trailer, Mong could only support his dramatic account by pointing to the state's evidence, blankets spotted with a little blood of unknown origins and found twenty-five feet deep in the strip-mine trash pit. He also neglected to mention that those blankets were never connected to Johnston.

The gory mutilations of Todd's corpse were clear evidence of Johnston's hatred for Todd, Mong claimed. "The intensity of that dislike [was] so eloquently portrayed in the brutal mutilation of his torso. Not merely shot, but ripped apart," he said.

Mong made the flat statement that Johnston had returned to Logan to bury the dismembered corpses. It didn't seem to matter that the only evidence to support that claim was the infamous footprint in the riverbank and a feed sack—similar to the type used by Johnston and practically every other farmer in the Hocking Hills—found near the railroad track. He didn't offer any answers to the obvious questions raised by this scenario. Why would Johnston run such a high risk of detection by going back to town? How could he do it without leaving a trace of evidence in his truck?

In this case, a hint of incest trumped the need for evidence. And Mong would more than hint at incest, as he reached the crescendo of his closing argument. "Incest, like rape, is not a sexual occurrence, but it is one of, indeed, abuse and dehumanization and violence," Mong orated. "And when the threat of exposure, when all else has failed, and you can't take any more of it, and when you are telling somebody, 'This is it, give me the car, leave me alone, or I'll tell them what you are really like, just like when I asked the chaperone, Should I tell the truth?' I am going to tell the truth, and so the ultimate form of incest is murder."

Suhr offered an entirely different scenario in his summation. He reminded the judges of all the evidence that the killings had actually taken place in the cornfield in the early evening. None of the people who'd heard the shots were related or connected to anyone involved in the case. But their statements presented a problem for the police: They needed to identify the killer in a big hurry, and they had no suspect handy for a scenario where the killings happened in the cornfield. But they did have a stepfather, and in that climate of fear, he would have to do.

"You can't have a city like Logan, a county like Hocking, going around worried out of their minds, as some of the testimony has indicated, about some person or persons that would do that to people," Suhr said. "So, right away, right away a decision was made that, that Dale Johnston, it had to be him. They have got a scapegoat, and they don't go off half-cocked. That's what happened in this case."

He asserted that the key elements of the state's theory of the crime simply made no sense. No one who testified suggested there had ever been any arguments between Todd and Dale Johnston regarding the orange Skyhawk. The only mention of a fight over the car had been made by Mong during his closing argument. Todd may have wanted the car, and he apparently needed money for some reason, but there was nothing in evidence to dispute that everyone in the Johnston household was in accord over the car. There was nothing to fight over, certainly nothing to kill for.

Similarly, Mong had conjured up Annette's supposed threat to expose her stepfather, Suhr said. If she had indeed told others that Dale Johnston had molested her, to the point of casually dropping the accusation into a lunch conversation with strangers, what was left to expose?

Suhr pointed to the previously introduced letter Annette had written to a friend days before her death as strong evidence that Annette was not fearful of sexual abuse by Johnston. To the contrary, Annette was upset over matters of sexual etiquette in the Schultz household. In the letter, Suhr noted, Annette wrote that Sandy had ordered her to get out of the house because Sandy had discovered that her husband Don had allowed the young couple to use his apartment as a place to have sex.

He ended by reminding the judges that the Schultzes were not the only grieving parents in the courtroom. "Dale and Sarah have lost a child, but they have the additional grief of being wrongfully charged that they were somehow involved," he said.

The arguments were over by lunchtime, and after the break, the judges issued a warning before they began their deliberations. When they returned with their verdict, no outbursts would be tolerated.

It was all over in plenty of time for everyone to get home in time for dinner. After a seventeen-day-long trial, the three judges reached their verdict in less than four hours of deliberation.

When they reconvened the trial, the spectator seats were, for the first time since the show began, mostly empty. All but a few of the people on the pine benches had taken the warning to heart, though they hadn't gone far. A crowd of about a hundred people gathered in a cluster on the first floor of the courthouse—just about where they had queued up in the cold at the start of the trial. There they could listen together to a live broadcast of the trial on a local radio station.

When Stillwell announced the first verdict—"Guilty"—there was near-total silence in the court. Johnston was grim-faced, stunned. Tyack silently mouthed his unbelieving reaction: "What was it?"

The only sounds in the court were the ghoulish cheers coming from the offstage choir of the vengeful folks of Logan. At the announcement of the second verdict—"Guilty"—the people whooped once more.

Sentence would be imposed another day, but no one in Logan doubted that it would be anything but death. All that remained was for the court to instruct Sheriff Jones to take any additional measures necessary to ensure the safety of the defendant. The defense team was provided with a police escort out of Hocking County.

—6—

ONE CONVICTED, THREE SENTENCED

Noises in the dark brought Sarah Johnston and her loaded shotgun to her front porch. There was a man moving around the property, and she was living alone in the trailer—the same trailer that had been proven, to the satisfaction of three judges and many of the people of Logan, to be the scene of the murders of her daughter and her daughter's boyfriend. Sarah had not returned by choice. She had nowhere else to go; it was her home, and she'd be damned if she'd tolerate any more skulking about by the people who'd ruined her life.

The murder of her daughter had been just the start of her accelerating spiral into fear, suspicion, and anger. Her husband was an inmate on death row, her stepson was away on duty with the US Marines, and her other daughter had been taken from her by the state and tossed into the foster-care system. She herself was living under repeated threats of being indicted as an accomplice or even a participant in the killings—tragedy compounded by horror. Her family retreat in the isolated, lush Hocking Hills had become, for her, a prison with trees.

The prowler had a badge and a familiar face. Sarah recognized him as Jim Thompson, the Logan Police Department detective who had led the investigation that resulted in Dale's conviction. Dale was at least free from Thompson; Sarah was not. "He was always following me, sneaking around," Sarah said.

Sarah's paranoia was based on a legitimate fear. They really were out to get her. Police and prosecutors had directly, though not officially, accused her of taking part in the dismemberment of the bodies after Dale had shot them. Their theory was that Sarah had taken a class to learn how to butcher the rabbits they raised to sell for meat; she clearly would have been able to apply those skills to the carving of the corpses. Then, according to the police accusations, she and her other daughter Michelle were supposed to have helped Dale put the body parts into animal feed sacks, which Dale took back to the edge of downtown Logan for disposal and burial.

Had she actually done anything even remotely close to the actions attributed to her in the local whispering campaign, she really would have been as crazy as the prosecutors were trying to make her out to be. "I don't know how anybody in their right mind could have killed those kids, let alone cut them up like that," she said.

Sarah would in fact soon lose her grip on sanity. Within a few months, she would be taken in handcuffs to a state mental hospital. But on that night, she was clearheaded enough to know that Jim Thompson was trespassing on her property.

"What are you doing?" she shouted out to the prowler. Thompson retorted defiantly that he was on police business. She demanded to see a warrant, but he contended he didn't need one.

Sarah ended the conversation by firing a load of birdshot in Thompson's general direction. "I didn't think I'd hit him, but later it got back to me that he had to fly out to California after that, and he had a hard time sitting down," she said. Thompson never made an official report on the incident, nor did he ever charge her with assaulting a police officer, she said.

Ever since the first days after the discovery of the bodies, Sarah knew that Dale was the prime and only suspect. "We lived sort of an odd lifestyle out in the country. Dale was somebody they could pin it on," she said.

She knew how intent the authorities were on getting a conviction of Dale but, like him, she believed the truth would prevail at the trial, and the mess would be straightened out. Once the verdict was handed down, though, she was totally unprepared for its impact. On the morning of the last day of the trial, she went to Logan to have breakfast at the little downtown restaurant where she'd eaten with Dale's attorneys on most mornings of the trial days. The owner had treated them kindly, she recalled. She had not been inside the courtroom during the trial, except for her testimony. As a witness, she was barred by rule from attending the trial sessions.

She could have gone into the courtroom for the reading of the verdict, but something about the mood of the courthouse crowd—nearly giddy with anticipation of a death sentence—told her to stay where she was. She could see the courthouse from the restaurant, and when the people erupted in cheers, she knew what had happened. "I just went stone cold," she said. This cold would not pass, however. It was more like a quick freeze that locked a fierce anger into her heart.

After the trial, Sarah went to the Columbus area to stay with Dale's mother, Blanche Messick, but that arrangement lasted only a few weeks.

With nowhere else to go, she returned to the trailer on Trowbridge Road. The property deeds had been signed over to Dale's attorneys, but they allowed her to stay on.

There was a macabre sort of welcome wagon waiting for her. Every time a new grand jury was called in Hocking County, the rumor mill flashed the news of Sarah's imminent indictment.

"I lived in total dread," she said. "I knew if they could convict Dale, they could convict me." In this time of high anxiety, Sarah said, she drank more than she should have. "I decided if I was going to die, I might as well go out in a blaze of glory," she said.

Her sense of dread was intensified when anonymous callers scorched her ears with ugly messages such as "You're worse than he is," or "You knew what was going on. Why didn't you stop it?" Other callers would simply play recordings of gunshots.

In the woods around her house, there were people watching her, Sarah believed. She could hear them signaling by making birdcalls. Sometimes, it seemed they wanted her to know they were out there because they were making the calls of birds that were nowhere near Ohio at that time of the year.

Anyone who tried to be decent to her was also harassed, she said. People who came out to visit her were frequently pulled over by police and questioned as soon as they left the trailer, she said.

Her attempts to land and hold a job were a series of caustic failures. She tried using her maiden name, but people found out anyway. One prospective employer rejected her, saying, "You're that convicted killer's wife, aren't you?" She managed to get a job in retail sales, but her supervisor let her go after only a few days, saying he regretted having to take the action, but he was "under pressure." Sarah was sure she knew who was exerting the pressure—the same group of Logan power brokers who had orchestrated the murder investigation and the trial.

"I was alone, I was harassed," she said. "I wasn't really crazy, I was just so dadgone angry and frustrated." She became convinced that most of what was happening to her was part of a calculated campaign of intimidation. "Whoever was responsible for the cover-up wanted to keep me scared and out of the way," she said.

She went into psychological counseling and took some vocational courses, knowing that they'd probably never help her get a job. She was also having a difficult time holding things together at the farm. Someone burned down the framework of the house that Dale had started to build for them. She couldn't afford to feed the livestock, so she started to sell off the animals, even the pets. "Oh, God, it hurt to get rid of those dogs," she said. She did manage to keep Dale's favorite horse, an Appaloosa; the animal lived till the age of twenty-six.

One way to push the bile back down her throat was to try to help with Dale's appeal efforts. Sympathetic people would come to her and tell her things, and she would pass them on to the attorneys and try to check out the tips herself.

A young woman who'd been a close friend of Annette's—close enough to lend her an evening dress for the finals of the Miss Parade of the Hills pageant competition—told Sarah a shocking story of drug use and distribution among the upper echelons of Logan society. The woman said she knew Dale hadn't murdered Todd and Annette. The killings were drug-related, but the investigators were deliberately avoiding that angle, the young woman said, because some important people in town were involved in the illegal trafficking. She knew this, she said, because she worked at a local nursery and floral shop that was an important part of the drug pipeline.

There was a strange sales pattern at the nursery, the woman said. At a certain time of the month, there would be a rush of calls from people ordering a particular floral arrangement. These arrangements all had the same order code, and each had a package labeled "fertilizer" attached to the vase. The woman strongly suspected the packages actually contained drugs. Some of the customers who ordered that arrangement were involved in the case against Dale Johnston, she said.

The woman had left the nursery about a month before telling the story to Sarah. When Sarah went to check the place out, she found the business had been shut down and abandoned.

Her conspiracy theories were solidified by information from other tipsters. In 1985, a friend of hers named Rusty, who was a practicing "white witch" among the neopagan Wiccan advocates in the southeast Ohio area, told her he knew of something evil in the heart of Logan. There was, Rusty said, a satanic-style cult that included leading businessmen and members of the justice system in Logan.

More confirmation came from a woman who worked in the Hocking County Courthouse. The woman prefaced her story by saying she would never repeat it in public, but she had learned that the murders of Todd and Annette were directly related to the local drug culture. Todd was the primary target, the woman said, and Annette was killed simply because she was there.

All of this information was useless legally. Years later, though, it would look less like rumor and more like the truth.

Sarah started to think of ways she could act on her suspicions. She learned that some of the people she suspected were part of a group that held irregular meetings. When she found out the time and place of one of those meetings, she concocted a plan to take revenge on her enemies. She made some inquiries about obtaining explosives. What she wanted to do was blow up the meeting place while the members of the group were inside; if any survived, she would be there to pick them off with her rifle.

She never acted on her plan, but she did tell her counselor about it during a therapy session in the fall of 1985. She was trying to tell him about the dark places her mind was racing to in those days. "I didn't care about anything anymore," she said.

As soon as he heard about the violent scheme, the counselor excused himself, saying, "I have to make some calls." Sarah left his office and went off to some other errands.

She didn't get far. She was arrested by police and handcuffed. She was involuntarily committed to a state mental hospital, under an order signed by Frederick Mong, one of the prosecutors at Dale's trial, who had by then been made a judge.

At the hospital, Sarah made the commitment look like a wise move. "I was plain defiant. I tore up the administrative office," she said. Her stay lasted about three months, and she was placed on lithium, a drug often used in the treatment of bipolar disorder. She was advised that if she wanted to stay sane, she needed to leave Hocking County.

By this time, there was no more fight left in Sarah. "They tried to drive me crazy for three years, and they finally did it," Sarah said. She did everything she could to leave her past behind. She divorced Dale, remarried a quiet, re-clusive man, and moved with him to his family's farm near the Ohio River.

Dale's demons, by contrast, were all too real, as real as the steel of the bars of his death row cell. But he decided he couldn't allow himself to descend into despair and anger. Instead, he became determined to go in the direction implied in the Samuel Johnson aphorism: "The prospect of being hanged fo-cuses the mind wonderfully."

He focused on getting himself out of prison. In doing this, he refused to abandon his faith in the justice system. All the toxic fog of vicious lies would be cleared away, he believed, and everyone would see that he was the victim of a terrible miscarriage of justice.

Of course, he had clung to that belief ever since he had been made a sus-pect. Looking back, Johnston said, his faith had been wildly misplaced. "I was dumb and naïve and trusted in the justice system," he said.

That naïveté had led him to make a series of missteps, essentially deliver-ing himself into the hands of his enemies. Chief among those errors was his decision to come into the Logan Police Department for the interrogation that police mined for evidence against him. He walked into the trap believ-ing that police regarded him as someone who could help with the investiga-tion. "I was still hopeful," he said. "I was going on the assumption they were honest and conducting a legitimate investigation."

Now, Dale is convinced that Thompson's request to assist in producing a sketch of someone who might have relevant information was just a ruse. In hindsight, he can also see that Thompson was using the presence of Ohio Bureau of Investigation Det. Herman Henry to help sell the charade. While Henry was working with Dale on the sketch, Thompson was lurking silently in the interrogation room, waiting to pounce.

After Thompson started lashing out with his accusations of murder and incest, Dale could have walked out at any time, but he did not. He assumed he was under arrest, but he also stayed because he thought his repeated claims of his innocence might eventually get through to Thompson. Dale was advised of his right to remain silent, but he waived it, comfortable in the belief that he had nothing to hide. Dale claimed he never said the things that Thompson would later testify that he had said. But that was an essential part of Thompson's plan: to make it his word against Dale's.

"They could've videotaped it, but if they had, they would've been bound by what I said. They intentionally failed to make a record of it," Dale said.

As the investigation increasingly pressed in on him, Dale wrote to the Ohio attorney general to complain about the tactics of the local police. He never received a response.

Other than that, he said, all he could do was to watch helplessly as he was being fitted for the hangman's noose. "There was nothing I could do about it," he said.

There was little he could do about his deteriorating financial situation, either. He was forced to stop work on the home he was building on his property, the deed to which had been signed over to his attorneys. He was also unable to take on outside contracting work. "Knowing they might arrest me at any time, there was no way I could go out and contract with somebody to build them a house," he said.

For the most part, his neighbors did not join in the clamor to blame him for the murders. "They were typical hill people. They kept to themselves and minded their own business, but the ones who knew me supported me," he said. One neighbor, Ralph Cherry, got tired of the frequent visits from police officers who were trying to extract some information from him to use against Johnston. Cherry told them to stop coming out and asking him the same questions.

The case progressed relentlessly, each step confirming Dale's advance reservation at a prison cell. He was arrested, bail was denied, and he spent four months in the county jail awaiting trial. Through all of that, Dale persisted in believing his innocence would eventually become apparent to all. "I thought once it came to trial, the truth would come out," he said.

At the end of the trial, Dale thought his faith in the system had been validated. The three judges would certainly see through the flimsy case presented by the prosecution, he thought. Wrong again. "When I heard the judge say

'Guilty,' I couldn't believe it. I was in shock," he said. "I was thinking, things like this happen in Russia, not here, not in the United States."

The shock wore off the moment he arrived at the maximum-security prison in Lucasville, Ohio. He received the standard humiliation of being stripped and deloused. Then he was marched through a series of doors that locked behind him. When he came to the death row cell block, the other inmates were "pressed up against the doors of their cells, wanting to see the new guy. They were all pale, like zombies," he said. "I can still hear that cell door slamming," he said.

The hardest thing to accept, he said, was the total loss of control. He'd always set his own schedules, plotted his own paths. "Inside, you can make no decisions on your own. Whatever you did was under someone else's control," he said.

Then there was the bleak monotony of prison life. "I was always an outdoors guy. The only times I came inside on the farm were when it stormed or when there was nothing else to do . . . and there was always something else to do."

Living on death row meant accepting that your next-door neighbor is a convicted killer. To have any sort of personal interactions, adjustments had to be made in the sort of person you chose to associate with. For example, some inmates were allowed to cut the hair of other inmates. One of the men who sometimes trimmed Dale's hair was Bill Wickline, the dismemberment specialist who had been hiding out near Logan at the time of Todd and Annette's murders.

Of all the thoughts racing through Dale's mind, one dominated his thinking: "Well, you got kicked in the teeth pretty good. What're you gonna do now?"

Dale was determined to avoid becoming part of the zombie brigade. He joined a circle of newspaper readers, inmates who would share the local newspapers they got from their hometowns. This way, he was able to read five or six newspapers a day.

He also read the Bible. "I was a late-comer to the Lord," he said. He maintained his relationship with the local pastor who'd presided over the memorial service for Annette and who'd become a family friend. He read the Book of Job many times.

As closely as he read anything else, he read the 1,200-page transcript of his trial. He used it to create timelines of his movements, as well as those of other key characters in the case. By sifting through the testimony, he hoped to be able to determine the identity of the two men he'd been talking to when Sarah and Michelle came home on the evening Todd and Annette disappeared.

He was fairly certain either that the two men were Harold Summers, the boss of the strip-mining operation on Johnston's land, and his foreman; or that the two were his neighbor Ralph Cherry and Ralph's son John. He found something in the transcript that allowed him to eliminate the two mining company men. Summers had testified that he had not been in Hocking County the week of the murders, and the mining operation had been shut down.

That meant it had to be the Cherrys. But how could he prove it? Ralph Cherry had testified that he couldn't recall anything significant about Monday, October 4, so he couldn't state that he'd had a conversation with Dale that particular evening. At first, Dale couldn't remember anything of significance, either. But when he pressed his memory, he recalled one minor detail of a conversation that might have been on the evening in question. Ralph had been a bit upset with his son John, Dale recalled, because John had been late in coming out to the farm to help his father.

It wasn't much, but Dale gave the information to his attorneys. Knowing there were people on the outside working to gain his release helped to keep his spirits up and his faith strong. That, and the very real prospect of being the recipient of a lethal injection, kept his mind wonderfully focused on vindication and freedom.

The worst moments, the times when his faith was most severely tested, were not when he thought about his execution. What really bothered him, frightened him, was thinking of how he'd be remembered, if that day ever came. He would always be a maniacal killer, someone who'd butchered the young woman who looked to him as her father. "What would my legacy be, knowing I was innocent, but being convicted of killing my own kid?" he said. "My other kids would have people say to them, 'Oh, your Dad was executed.'"

The forgotten victim in the Johnston family was Michelle, Annette's younger sister. She suffered nearly as much as her mother or her stepfather, yet they at least were adults who had access to attorneys. At the age of sixteen, Michelle was removed from her home by the state, subjected to marathon hostile interrogation sessions, and hauled into juvenile court as a criminal defendant. Over and over, she told the authorities that she had no knowledge of the crime, which happened to be the truth. Nevertheless, she was the target of a long campaign of legally sanctioned spite—all because she refused to lie for the state.

During the months after the murders, Michelle gave several statements to the authorities. Each time she swore she saw no violence at the Johnston trailer that night, that Todd and Annette were not there, and nothing out of the ordinary happened.

But when the strong right arm of the law grabbed Dale, the other arm sucker punched Michelle. A few days before Dale was indicted in September 1983, a Hocking County sheriff's deputy and a state Child Protective Services caseworker came into Michelle's high-school classroom and ordered her to come with them. "They tried to be friendly and chatty, but they wouldn't tell me where they were taking me," Michelle said. She wasn't allowed to call her mother. She was detained until she was picked up by the first of four sets of foster parents she would have over the next two years. "Each home was worse than the previous one," she said.

The only explanation given to Sarah for having a second daughter taken from her was that Michelle was being removed from the Johnston home "for her own safety." The clear implication was that Michelle was a potential witness against Dale, so allowing her to live in the same home with him might subject her to harm. No one offered an explanation as to why, if Michelle were in any danger, the state hadn't acted sooner. After all, it had been about eleven months since Dale had been made the sole suspect in the killings, and Michelle had lived with him all that time.

Although the forced removal of Michelle from her home did nothing to improve her safety or welfare, it was a great leap forward for the prosecution. By making Michelle a ward of the state, it put her under the control of the people who were trying to construct a capital murder case against Dale. Those people had a deep, pressing need for her to change her story supporting Dale's alibi, and they weren't queasy about trampling on the rights of a minor child, if that's what it took.

What it took to get something close to what they wanted was to force Michelle to endure repeated interrogation sessions, conducted by police and prosecutors and lasting up to six hours. By law, a legal guardian was appointed for Michelle during this period. In practice, however, the guardian became an agent of the prosecution.

"The interrogations I was subjected to were cruel, and my court-appointed guardian sold me out," Michelle said. "Basically, he let them do whatever they wanted to me mentally."

Michelle's descriptions of her interrogations are strikingly similar to Dale's descriptions of his: long, grueling, repetitious, and relentless. Over and over, her interrogators demanded that she admit that she'd seen the murders; over and over, she denied witnessing anything other than an unremarkable night at home with her parents.

"They tried to distort everything I said," Michelle said. They hammered her unmercifully on the issue of Dale's possession of a handgun. Since the prosecution had no murder weapon, it was vital to their case to show that Dale possessed a weapon that might have been used in the murders. A few state witnesses had given statements that they'd seen Dale with a handgun, but more defense witnesses would testify that he had no such gun, and those witnesses were in the Johnston home much more frequently. The prosecutors needed a statement from Michelle to tip the balance in their direction. Jim Thompson even tried to hypnotize her with a pencil during the interrogations, she said.

However, Michelle refused to give them what they wanted because she'd never seen her stepfather with a handgun and had never seen one in their home. The truth was not what her interrogators wanted. They showed her a picture that police had taken in the Johnston home, showing a black tool grip protruding from underneath some other items. They repeatedly insisted this was a handgun. Michelle repeatedly refused to agree with them. As it turned out, the object was the grip of a handsaw.

For refusing to bend the truth to fit the prosecution's scenario, Michelle was slapped with a juvenile court indictment charging her with seven counts of perjury. As spurious as they were, the charges made a fine lever for the prosecutors to use to pry Michelle away from her support of Dale's alibi.

Although Michelle was never tried on the perjury charges, the prosecutors had gained what they saw as a tactical advantage. Their accusations had branded her as an accused liar, so the prosecutors could argue that she was lying to protect her mother and stepfather.

"I had seven perjury charges against me and was labeled a hostile witness, simply because I wouldn't say what they wanted me to say—which was that I watched Mom and Dale murder Todd and Annette in our kitchen!" Michelle said.

Michelle's refusals to lie for the state caused her interrogators to intensify the pressure on her. She finally devised a way to get them to back off a bit. She started telling her questioners that she couldn't remember anything about that evening or night. The last thing she could recall was getting picked up at the clinic by her mother, she told them. It was as much as the prosecution was going to get from Michelle, so they tried to make it work for them. At the trial, the prosecutors claimed, without any supporting medical evidence, that Michelle's inability to recall anything from that night was due to a bad case of "hysterical amnesia," caused by her witnessing the terrible murders.

It was a tortured bit of reasoning used to justify the mental torture of a teenager. But it worked.

After the verdict, Michelle was shipped to another foster home. She was cut off from contact with her mother. Against her wishes, her caseworkers ordered her to enroll in a mechanic-training course.

On the second anniversary of the murders, Michelle said, one of her fellow students taunted her, asking, "Killed anybody today?" She fired back, saying, "No, but you could be the first."

As soon as she turned eighteen and thus grew out of the foster care system, Michelle moved back in with Sarah. But life in the trailer on Trowbridge Road would never be the same for either of them. Sarah was sliding out of emotional control, and Michelle was her caretaker.

After Sarah was committed to the mental hospital, Michelle continued to live in the trailer. It was a lonely place to be, and one visitor in particular brought no solace. The prosecutor's chief investigator, who'd been one of Michelle's interrogators, dropped by for a brief but bitter chat. Michelle said the investigator asked her to give him the rifle and shotgun that were inside the house. Once again, the state was only trying to look out for Michelle's safety. The investigator asked for the weapons, Michelle said, because he suggested that Sarah might use them to do something crazy, maybe even shooting the pets that remained on the farm. Michelle told him the only people she needed protection from were men wearing badges. She kept the weapons and told the investigator to get out.

After Sarah was released and moved away from Hocking County, Michelle went with her. Both Sarah and Dale now say that the way Michelle was treated was more vicious and cruel than what they suffered.

Michelle had a one-word assessment of what the people in power did to her: "Outrage."

—7—

FREE IS A FOUR-LETTER WORD

The gangly, grey-haired man sipping a beer at a back table at the Home Tavern was an undercover operative in his own hometown. Bud Walker, a semi-retired investigator, had taken on the highly unpopular mission of trying to prove the innocence of a convicted dismemberment murderer. At least he wasn't an outsider; he'd grown up in the Hocking Hills. He listened to the bar talk and drove the back roads, seeking someone to lead him to the truth he knew was buried somewhere in Logan.

Walker wondered why the police had worked so hard to ignore what was obvious to him—that Todd and Annette had been killed by someone they encountered after their walk down the C&O tracks into West Logan. In fact, the police hadn't seemed interested at all in the victims. "It was like those kids stepped out of a vacuum and got themselves killed," Walker said.

The trial testimony had offered only sketchy portraits of Todd and Annette. Todd was presented by the prosecution as Annette's unfortunate boyfriend, who happened to be with her when her jealous stepfather's rage exploded. Annette was just the beauty-pageant contestant who sometimes dropped casual hints about some dark deeds that occurred in the trailer on Trowbridge Road. Walker found people who told him about Annette's dark side, saying she'd been found having sex with a Logan police officer in the back seat of his cruiser; that officer later had a role in the early investigation of her murder but resigned from the force soon afterwards. She may also have made sex tapes with some well-known men in town.

Of more direct import to Johnston's appeal efforts, Walker succeeded in taking the couple's trail a step further than the police had. He found a woman in West Logan who remembered Todd and Annette as the young couple who'd come up to her yard sale on the evening of their deaths. They put a five-dollar deposit on a small coffee table, which, as far as the woman could recall, they would use to furnish an apartment where they planned to move.

This bit of information was another hole shot into the state's case. If the woman at the yard sale was telling the truth—and there was no discernable reason to doubt her—Todd and Annette were furniture shopping at just about the same time when the prosecutors alleged they were being abducted by Dale Johnston. The woman's description of the seemingly carefree young couple was in stark contrast to the prosecution's portrayal of the victims as fearful, intimidated teenagers.

Whether the woman's story might have made a difference at the trial is an unanswerable question, but Walker's other major discovery was documented and not open to interpretation. He established the identity of the men Johnston had been talking to at his farm on the evening of the murders, thus confirming Johnston's alibi.

All it took was the sort of simple investigative legwork that any professional police detectives should have done right at the start. After using his time in prison to refine his memory, Johnston had become convinced that the men were almost certainly his neighbor Ralph Cherry and Cherry's son John.

Ralph Cherry had died before Walker started his inquiries. Walker reinterviewed John Cherry, but Cherry could not fix a date to the conversation. But when Walker passed on Johnston's recollection that the elder Cherry had been upset with his son that day, something clicked in John Cherry's memory.

Yes, John recalled, he'd been late coming out to the farm that day. That's why his father was ticked off, because he'd expected him to come earlier in the day and help him with some farm chores. At that point, John Cherry still couldn't remember the date, but he did remember why he was late—it was because he'd taken a load of grain to be ground at a nearby mill, and the grinding had taken longer than he expected.

There would have to be a record of that transaction, and Walker went to the mill to find it. The operators of the mill gave him access he needed, and as soon as he located the right ledger book, he found exactly what he was looking for: an entry stating that John Cherry had brought grain to be milled on Monday, October 4, 1982.

For further confirmation, Cherry went through his personal financial records and found the check he'd written to the millers on Monday, October 4, 1982.

Now it wasn't just Sarah and Michelle saying nothing out of the ordinary happened that evening on the Johnston farm. Johnston's alibi was now supported by an affidavit signed by John Cherry, stating that he was having a routine conversation with Dale Johnston at about the same time that the state alleged that Johnston was in the trailer, murdering his stepdaughter and her boyfriend.

Walker was convinced that this new evidence would crack the state's case beyond repair. He was only partly right, but that does not diminish his contribution to the effort to get to the truth of these crimes. Walker would never have been given the assignment were it not for the person who hired him, Johnston's co-counsel, Bob Suhr.

After the conviction, Suhr could easily have dropped Johnston as a client. Johnston had been pauperized by the trial. He couldn't pay Suhr a nickel. The state would have provided a court-appointed attorney for Johnston's appeal, but Suhr stayed on the case. He didn't think it was right to abandon Johnston; besides, he was certain beyond a reasonable doubt that Johnston was, in fact, innocent.

"If it wasn't for Bob Suhr and Bud Walker, I wouldn't be alive today," Johnston said.

Johnston's fortified alibi was just one piece of legal buckshot for what the defense believed was a fully loaded appeal of the conviction.

They also offered a detailed alternative scenario of the murders, featuring Tex Meyers as the primary villain. They used all the background information Suhr and Walker had accumulated on Tex—his obsession with Annette, his proclivity for knife play, his talk of cult activities, and his flight from the Logan area as soon as he was questioned by police. They argued that Tex was the man Shirley Frazier said she had seen arguing with a young couple on the railroad tracks. She said she'd seen the three go down the railroad-track embankment, and then heard shots followed by a female scream and more shots, and then a man wearing a cowboy hat skulked away. When the truth emerged, Frazier's account was proven accurate, though the killer turned out to be someone other than Tex.

The list of alleged trial errors also included the entire testimony of Steve Rine, the witness of the phantom abduction, as well as the hearsay testimony of Annette's statements that she had been sexually abused by her stepfather, and the prosecutors' violation of the rules of discovery by failing to provide the defense with the statements of numerous witnesses whose statements indicated that the killings had taken place near the cornfield, not at the Johnston trailer.

This shotgun approach worked because the appellate court's decision blasted the prosecutors and the trial court with both barrels.

On the issue of the violation of discovery rules, the appellate court's decision stated, "We must conclude that the statements in question were withheld from appellant during trial."

This prosecutorial maneuver clearly undermined the defense's ability to present an alternative theory of the crime at trial, the court ruled. "We find these items of evidence can clearly be interpreted to indicate that the killings might have taken place at the cornfield, rather than at the appellant's home," the ruling stated.

In particular, the withheld statement from the worker who was frightened by the strange noises he heard coming from the cornfield on the night of the murders was possible evidence of multiple people participating in the aftermath of the murders, the court held. "The statement describing voices in the same area in the predawn hours of the next morning supports an inference that more than one person was involved in this phase of the crime. Such evidence, if believed by the fact-finders, would certainly have a bearing on the fact-finders' deliberations. The state's case, after all, was entirely circumstantial," the ruling stated.

Regarding the statements that cast suspicion on Tex Meyers, the high court ruled that the trial court and the prosecutors had all erred. The prosecutors had been wrong in withholding statements that could have implicated Meyers, and they erred in accepting the police investigators' conclusion that Meyers had nothing to do with the case. "We rule that appellant's request for information implicating any person other than the defendant specifically included such information, regardless of the prosecutor's own interpretation of the data," the ruling stated.

The appellate court was unsparing and unequivocal in its criticism of the trial court on this issue. "We reject outright the trial court's rationale that such evidence should not be considered. A defendant on trial for his life certainly has the right to introduce evidence that the crime was committed by someone else," the ruling stated.

In its brief contesting the appeal, the prosecution conceded that the testimony about what other people heard Annette say about what might have occurred between her and her stepfather was a clear violation of the rules against hearsay testimony. But, the prosecution contended, it was validly admitted at trial because it tended to support the prosecution's contention that Annette was afraid of Johnston.

However, the higher court thoroughly disposed of that argument. "We note that this theory of admission was not presented to the trial court," the appellate court stated. "Furthermore, the relevance of this theory of admission of the highly inflammatory statements alleging incest is so tenuous, if it exists at all, that admission under this theory would be outweighed by the prejudicial impact of the factual content of Annette's statements."

While it might be reasonable to argue that a victim of sexual abuse would likely be afraid of the abuser, the court stated, to apply that general assumption to this case would mean having "to accept as true the fact that the incest occurred." "This, in turn, would require that we accept the hearsay as true, in violation of the hearsay rule. The statements are not admissible under this theory," the ruling stated.

Perhaps the harshest personal criticism in the ruling was directed at the scandalous and unsupported accusations made by prosecutor Frederick Mong in his closing argument. "The state did exploit the prejudicial value of the nature of Annette's allegations in its closing argument, referring to murder as 'the ultimate form of incest,'" the ruling stated. "This is an improper reference to evidence not of record, and would probably support reversal in a jury trial."

However, the appeals court gave the trial court some credit—too much credit, in retrospect—for being able to avoid being improperly influenced by Mong's overwrought attempt to connect rumors of improper sexual advances with the reality of two horrible murders. "Confusion of the issues or misleading the jury are not appropriate concerns in this trial to a panel of three experienced trial judges," the ruling stated. "Unfair prejudice is also much less likely to interfere with the judgment of such a panel."

In other words, the appellate court assumed that the three trial judges were above being pushed into a guilty verdict by the atmosphere of public bloodlust in which the trial was conducted. The appellate court judges did not know about the stack of death threats the trial judges had received.

The ruling also emphatically consigned the testimony of Steve Rine, the only state witness to place Dale Johnston anywhere near the crime scene, to a legal black hole.

"Hypnotically induced memory enhancement is often criticized as a potential distorter of the accuracy of hypnotically retrieved memories," the court stated. "After hypnosis, the gap-filling inventions are indistinguishable from the subject's actual memory of the events in question."

This innate problem of using hypnosis to produce evidence becomes "more acute" when, as in this case, there is no record of what the witness says he or she remembered before being hypnotized, the ruling stated. "In this case, for example, we have only the incomplete summaries of the witness's statements. Clearly, the admission of this hearsay as evidence against appellant raises very serious questions about appellants' basic rights."

On top of all that, the court ruled, there was nothing to support Rine's testimony—pre- or posthypnosis. By allowing Rine to testify at all, the trial court erred "in that Rine's hypnotically induced testimony was admitted without even minimal demonstration of its reliability," the high court ruled. Belaboring what the appellate court saw as obvious, the ruling stated, "We find, under the facts of this case, Rine's testimony should not have been admitted."

The case against Dale Johnston had been exposed as a concoction of inept bungling and outright, perhaps deliberate, violations of some of the most basic concepts of American justice. The appellate court ruling slapped the prosecutors with several serious instances of misconduct: for complicity in withholding important information from the defense, for introducing gossip under the guise of evidence, and for making sensational but legally baseless accusations in the closing argument. It also called into question the competence, if not the integrity, of the trial court: for allowing all the hearsay into evidence, for totally mishandling the testimony of Steve Rine, and for refusing to allow the defense to make its argument that someone else killed Todd and Annette.

The conduct of the police investigators was not a matter brought to the consideration of the appellate court. However, its ruling clearly indicts practically every officer and police agency involved in the case. It was the police who brought the tainted evidence to the prosecutors, and it was the police who discarded so much evidence that pointed to Johnston's innocence.

The ruling tossed out the state's star witness, plus all the hearsay evidence that supported the state's theory of the motivation for the killings being an incest-fueled jealous rage.

The appellate court's terse, capital-letter conclusion: "REVERSED AND REMANDED FOR NEW TRIAL."

That should have been the end of the state's prosecution and persecution of Dale Johnston. It was not.

The Hocking County prosecuting attorney at the time, Charles Gerken, quickly appealed the ruling to the Ohio Supreme Court, which in March of 1988 upheld the order reversing the verdict. Not to be swayed by the evisceration of the prosecution's case, Gerken announced that Dale Johnston would be tried again for the murders.

This time, however, the proceedings would not be held in Hocking County's home court. The trial was moved to Franklin County, which includes the state capital of Columbus, and was assigned to retired Franklin County Judge William Gillie. This judge was not disposed to be an agent of the prosecutor.

In a pretrial hearing, Gillie tossed out what little remained of the evidence against Johnston. He ruled that Johnston's police interrogators, particularly Jim Thompson, had violated Johnston's rights throughout his prolonged interrogation in October of 1982. This meant that everything Thompson testified that Johnston had said during that interview—testimony that Johnston contended was mostly lies—would not be admitted at the second trial. In addition, everything that the police confiscated from Johnston during that interview and the subsequent search of his home were also thrown out.

That included Johnston's boots, which Thompson had falsely claimed were stained with blood and which the state claimed were used to make the infamous impressions at the riverbank. Consequently, the testimony of the self-proclaimed footprint expert, Louise Robbins, was also out.

Gillie's ruling was appealed and reviewed by the Franklin County Court of Appeals. That panel was as resolute as the previous appellate court had been in attacking the validity of the state's case.

"The methods employed (in the police interrogation of Johnston) are violative of the basic principle that ours is an accusatorial and not an inquisitorial system," stated Judge Dean Stansborough in the unanimous decision.

Stansborough concluded in his ruling that Thompson lied about the blood-stains on Johnston's boots as a ploy to confiscate them and later use them as evidence, the ruling stated. "The conduct of the police during the eight and one half hour session indicates a process of interrogation and an attempt to overbear [Johnston's] free will through coercive behavior. The state presented no legitimate reason for the length of the interrogation in this instance."

At this point, there was nothing left for Gerken to do but to dismiss all charges against Dale Johnston. It was all a matter of playing out a poor hand that had been dealt him by the first investigators and prosecutors, Gerken said, in a 2011 interview with the author.

Gerken said he proceeded with the retrial of Johnston even though he believed the case was weak, at best. "I had trial evidence that I knew was not valid," he said. Specifically, he had serious reservations about the hypnotized eyewitness and about the prosecution's footprint expert, he said. In addition, he said, the prosecution's scenario of Johnston kidnapping the victims in Logan, murdering them at his home, and then bringing the bodies back to Logan for burial "just didn't make sense."

Nevertheless, Gerken said, it was important in a legal sense for him to go forward with the charges again. He said he was confident that the trial judge would rule the evidence was inadmissible—which was exactly what happened. That way, the state would be able to reinstate the murder charges against Johnston if new evidence was ever found. Had he actually brought the case to trial at that time, he said, Johnston would very likely have been acquitted and thus would be immune from any future prosecution in the case.

His handling of this phase of the case had severe repercussions for him, Gerken said. Public officials and private individuals in Logan pressed him to refile the charges against Johnston, even after the dismissal. He resisted, because there was no evidence left to take to trial, he said.

When he was up for reelection in 1992, he was opposed by Stillwell, who came out of retirement and made the Johnston case the main issue of the campaign. Stillwell died before the election, which Gerken won.

The next election cycle, however, Gerken was defeated, and he believes his resistance to press the prosecution of Johnston was a significant factor in his departure from public office. "I'm still being ostracized," Gerken said.

Regarding Johnston's conviction for a crime he did not commit, Gerken said, "It's all a damn shame."

. . .

On May 11, 1990, almost seven years after Dale Johnston was arrested for the murders of Todd Schultz and Annette Johnston, the state of Ohio was forced to let him go free—but not without one last bit of ugliness. He had been transferred to the Licking County Jail in Newark, Ohio, during the pretrial process.

About an hour before the announced time of the release, the sheriff's office received an anonymous call from a man who claimed to be hidden somewhere in sight of the jail. The caller said he had a high-powered rifle and planned to shoot Johnston in the head the minute he stepped out of the jail.

Sheriff Gerry Billy was not going to allow an assassination at his jail. While a group of reporters and cameramen gathered outside the front entrance to the jail, one of Billy's deputies drove Johnston and his attorneys away, using the deputy's private car and a rear entrance.

So, the celebratory news conference was moved to later in the afternoon at Suhr's office in Columbus. The death threat and the backdoor getaway did not diminish Johnston's joy. "I feel fantastic. It's a beautiful day," he told the *Columbus Dispatch*. He also vowed to work to find his daughter's killer. Sarah Johnston Brown, who by then had remarried and moved away from Hocking County, came to Columbus to restate her support for Dale and her belief in his innocence.

Back in Logan, Don Schultz scoffed at that. "He knows who did it. *He* did it," Schultz told the Columbus paper. Sandy Schultz was equally adamant, saying, "We know Dale killed them. Three judges found him guilty."

Less than two years later, Gerken steadfastly defended Hocking County against Johnston's civil suit for wrongful imprisonment.

"Plaintiff has the burden of proving by a preponderance of the evidence that he did not commit the murders of Todd Schultz and Annette Johnston," Gerken argued. Typically, he continued, a wrongful imprisonment claim is supported by the confession of someone other than the originally convicted defendant. It would take fifteen more years, but that condition would eventually be met.

For the purposes of denying Johnston compensation for his death sentence and his nearly seven years in prison, however, Gerken argued that the county and the state owed him nothing. "The plaintiff cries for justice, but justice carries a double-edged sword."

Johnston's attorneys believed they had both edges of the sword covered. They introduced John Cherry's statement, in which he was able to pinpoint the date and time that he and his father had been talking with Johnston at Johnston's farm. It was roughly the same time the state had alleged Johnston was killing Todd and Annette.

Also, Janice Moyer, the woman who had lived near Homer Street near the access road leading down to the cornfield and the river, testified about the caravan of vehicles she'd seen going across the tracks on the night after Todd and Annette disappeared. She said she'd told her husband, "There's been something gone desperately wrong down in the cornfield." She testified she told all this to the police officer who came to her house shortly after the murders were discovered, but he answered, "I don't want to know what you've seen. I want to know have you seen these kids."

Showing that Johnston was ten miles away from the murder scene was not enough, nor was showing that a whole group of other potential subjects were having some sort of a weird gathering at that scene. After a one-day trial, the Hocking County judge hearing the suit decided in the spring of 1993 that Johnston should receive zero compensation for having his life ruined by the state.

Johnston did not allow this latest setback to stop him from getting his life back together. He had lost his family and nearly all his possessions, but he had the ability to work with his hands—and he was free. He moved in with his mother for the last three years of her life.

Bob Suhr gave Johnston an old pickup and some tools, which enabled Johnston to start to work as a handyman. "Bob even paid me for the work I did for him, even though I still owed him a fortune," Johnston said.

Johnston advertised his home repair services in a local newspaper, and within a year, he had acquired all the customers he could handle. He found a little church that suited him.

For the next fifteen years, the truth remained plowed under, like stalks of dead corn.

−8−

CRACKING THE DAM OF LIES

The two old cops just wouldn't let go. Rodney Robinson had left the Hocking County Sheriff's Office as a detective about three months before the murders. As soon as the bodies were found, Sheriff Jimmy Jones called and asked him to come back and work on the case. Four months later, Robinson resigned in disgust over the way the investigation was being handled.

Robinson convinced his friend Jim Powers, a Logan Police Department officer at the time, that Dale Johnston almost certainly had nothing to do with the killings. Later, Powers became a Hocking County sheriff's deputy. Before and after Johnston was convicted, Robinson and Powers never wavered in their belief that Johnston did not commit the murders. Over the years, they frequently discussed the case. If they were in a public place and either of them heard someone repeating the gossip about the "evil stepfather," they'd politely interrupt the conversation and offer some facts as an antidote.

Robinson's disillusionment with Hocking County justice began the day the body parts were found. At Jones's request, he came to the cornfield and brought a metal detector he sometimes used to search crime scenes. His first impression was that the cornfield and the riverbank area did not offer much potential for evidence gathering, mostly because the area had been heavily trampled by police officers that day and by volunteer searchers on the day before.

He was, however, able to make two significant observations. The absence of large amounts of blood, plus the trail through the cornstalks from the riverbank to the burial site in the cornfield, suggested to him that the dismemberments had occurred near the river. There was a stone outcropping at the river's edge near the end of the trail; if the bodies had been dismembered there, much of the blood would have been washed away by the river.

Secondly, Robinson observed obvious shovel marks around the places where the heads and limbs had been buried. These should have been at least photographed, but they were not. The use of shovels indicated the killer or killers had enough time to go somewhere and get the tools after the killings. It would have been highly unlikely, he thought, for the shooter to bring digging tools with him. More than likely, he deduced, someone with knowledge of that terrain had been involved with the killings and the burials.

Robinson was also able to make a personal assessment of the prime suspect, Dale Johnston. He and another deputy were questioning Dale and Sarah before Dale was taken to the long interrogation by Jim Thompson. The other deputy was waltzing around the key issue, asking Dale whether he'd had an "inappropriate" relationship with Annette. The Johnstons weren't quite sure what he was talking about.

Robinson cut through the euphemisms, asking, "Did you have sex with your daughter?"

The look of shock on the faces of both Dale and Sarah told Robinson what he needed to know. He was convinced they were being honest with him when they denied anything like that had taken place. His belief in Johnston's innocence put him in direct conflict with those running the investigation. No one in authority wanted to listen to him then. He happened to be right, and they were wrong, but that was of no consequence in 1982.

Despite having much more experience in homicide investigations than anyone else on the case, Robinson was disregarded and excluded from any control of the case. Even so, Robinson persisted. He spoke with Jill Wolfery, the operator of the Animal Crackers theme park, who told him of the suspicious behavior of her employee Tex Meyers.

Robinson went out to Animal Crackers and saw a man standing in a garage, cutting up some meat. "You Tex?" Robinson asked. When Meyers nodded yes, Robinson said, "I want to talk with you."

Meyers appeared agitated. Robinson asked if Meyers knew Annette, and Tex said he did. One of Annette's friends had introduced him to her at the Hocking County Fair of 1982. Meyers said Annette had been bugging him about helping her get a job at Animal Crackers.

At this point, Robinson cut the interview short and made an appointment with Tex to come in to the sheriff's office for further questioning. Robinson reported back to Jones that Meyers should be considered a suspect. "You want to bring that guy in right now," Robinson told his boss.

Jones was not the least bit interested in going down that road. "He gave us hell for pickin' on him (Meyers)," Robinson said. Jones protested there was no way Meyers could have been involved. "No. I know him. He comes from a good family," the sheriff said. Jones made it obvious to Robinson that "all he wanted was Johnston," Robinson said.

There were two Kevin Meyerses who became part of the investigation, Robinson later discovered. One Kevin Meyers worked as a meat cutter in a butcher shop in Logan, and this man was ruled out as a suspect, he said. However, a different Kevin "Tex" Meyers was the man who worked at the Animal Crackers ranch and the one whom Robinson had tracked down. Had Jones allowed Robinson to bring Tex Meyers in, the identity mix-up would have been resolved—and the man who could have provided a major break in the investigation could have been properly interrogated.

Tex Meyers did not wait for the police to get their act together. He left town in a big hurry. Robinson found an address in a neighboring county that Meyers had put on an application for a job at Animal Crackers. He went to what turned out to be Meyers's mother's home in the Buckeye Lake area, where he found Tex. Meyers agreed to talk with Robinson, but he wanted to go outside, away from the family.

Robinson advised Meyers of his rights and recorded the interview. Meyers admitted to knowing Annette well enough to have what he thought was a boyfriend-girlfriend relationship with her. "He admitted he was foolin' around with her," Robinson said. However, Meyers denied seeing her on the day of the murders—a statement that other witnesses would later say was false. Meyers also agreed to come back to the Hocking County Sheriff's Office for an interview and a polygraph examination.

But after he interviewed Tex at Buckeye Lake, Robinson said, Jones ordered him to stop pursuing the Tex Meyers angle to the investigation. Robinson said he believes Meyers left the area and went a few counties north to Licking County, where he had left his wife. A few years later Tex committed suicide, according to information given to Robinson by Licking County authorities.

While he remained a Hocking County deputy, Robinson became deeply disturbed by the way he saw evidence being handled. When a deputy claimed there'd been a breakthrough in the case—one of Todd's pubic hairs had been found in Dale Johnston's boot—Robinson became suspicious, because he knew how that boot had been obtained. Ohio BCI Det. Herman Henry had told him that Jim Thompson had falsely claimed to see bloodstains on the boot and confiscated it during his interrogation of Johnston.

When he learned that the police claimed to have found a print made by that same boot of Johnston's on the riverbank, Robinson's suspicions intensified. "I saw the first casting of the boot print from the riverbank, and it was really bad quality," Robinson said. "But then, all of a sudden, they had a clean one, after they took Johnston's boots."

By the spring of 1983, Robinson had had enough. He resigned. "I was too goddamn tired of the lies," Robinson said later.

In 2006, the case escalated from a preoccupation to an active, though unofficial, investigation for Powers and Robinson. By this time, Robinson had retired again from law enforcement, and Powers was the chief probation officer for the municipal court of Logan. The topic of the 1982 murders came up during a conversation between Powers and one of his probationers, a man named Jimmy Frasure. "You guys ought to take a look at Kenny," Powers said Frasure told him. The "Kenny" Frasure referred to was a friend of his, Kenny Linscott. "Everybody in West Logan thought Kenny was mixed up with him (Todd Schultz)," Frasure told Powers.

Frasure also informed Powers that shortly before the murders, he had loaned a .22 rifle to Linscott. When Linscott returned the weapon, the barrel was mangled, which seemed odd to Frasure, since he knew Linscott was an experienced hunter.

Powers and Robinson took this piece of information to the county coroner. Their thinking was to review the forensics of the gunshot wounds and the recovered bullets, to determine if it might be possible that a rifle, rather than a pistol, had been used in the killings. The coroner wasn't interested in dredging up the old case; besides, he remained firmly convinced that Dale Johnston was the killer.

To Robinson and Powers, though, this new lead was too promising to dismiss. Powers had an advantage in pursuing the case, in that both Kenny

Linscott and his then-estranged wife Judy were part of his probation case-load. During a meeting with Linscott, Powers brought up the 1982 murders. The topic visibly distressed Linscott. When Powers asked Linscott what he knew, or whether he had been involved in any way, Linscott did not respond with categorical denials. Instead, Linscott came up with a standard-issue dodge that Powers had often heard from habitual criminals. "You can't prove that!" Linscott shot back. When Powers suggested Linscott had the ability to cut up two corpses, Linscott answered enigmatically, saying, "You ever tried butchering a hog?"

There was one person who could help them cut through Linscott's eva-sions—his estranged wife Judy.

It wasn't as if Judy Linscott were hiding. At the time of the murders, she was Linscott's girlfriend, living with him in his parents' barracks-beige modu-lar home in West Logan, and the mother of their first child. She'd married him in 1983, stayed right there in West Logan with him, raising three more children, until she left him in 2006. At that time, she was also on probation for drug charges. Despite the canvassing by police in the West Logan neigh-borhood, no one had ever asked her if she knew anything about the killings.

That would have to wait a while longer. Judy was in a women's rehabilita-tion center, trying to deal with her drug problem.

Judy knew things, however. She suspected things. She never forgot, nor did her suspicions ever diminish, nor, however, did she ever marshal the courage to speak out.

Never a fairy tale, her life with Linscott ended not long after the death of their daughter Betty Jo. When she was twenty, Betty Jo swallowed a fatal dose of contraband drugs at her boyfriend's insistence after the car they were driving in was stopped by police. Judy blamed Kenny for instigating the drug run, and she left him. Kenny professed sorrow and had Betty Jo's name tat-tooed on his forearm.

The tattoo on Judy's upper arm—"Kenny's Chic"—was an unfortunate suggestion that she was still attached to the man who, she said, beat her and kept her stocked with narcotics throughout their marriage. It wasn't; the man she'd bounced to after leaving Kenny Linscott was also named Kenny. The second Kenny had turned out to be only a marginally better man, and a worse speller, than the first. At least he too was history now.

After that breakup, she spent a month in an intensive program at the Rural Women's Recovery Program in Athens, Ohio. She'd landed there after failing a couple of routine drug screening tests that had been a condition of her earlier probation on drug charges. Besides daily counseling and required attendance at AA meetings, she performed the sort of tasks that had previously been beyond her capacity, like keeping her room clean.

At forty-nine, Judy was still as trim as she'd been when she'd dropped out of high school. She still wore her brown hair like she had in her teenage years, long and straight, parted down the middle and reaching below her shoulders. When she smiled or spoke, the traces of her hard life became obvious, though, in the stains on her teeth and the rasp in her voice. She was a child of the Appalachian foothills, without the strength or the skills to escape.

All things considered, though, Judy was better than she'd been in years. The staff at the center had some misgivings about her meeting with Powers and his unofficial partner Rodney Robinson—residents were supposed to be focusing on moving toward a healthier future, not dredging up the demons of the past. But Judy was OK with it. She knew Powers and trusted him. He'd helped get her admitted to the center.

Powers believed Judy might know something important about the case, and now that she was strong enough to answer questions, he brought Robinson, who would take notes.

Robinson was seventy-five at the time, with more than forty-five years' experience as a law enforcement officer and with more than fifty homicide investigations to his credit. He had started his investigation at the cornfield crime scene, had watched as the lead investigator made a star witness out of a man whose testimony Robinson had discarded as worthless, had identified a key witness himself only to have his efforts dismissed by the sheriff. Now, the decades-cold trail had led him to this nondescript conference room at the rehab center.

Robinson and Powers told Judy the original investigation had traced Todd and Annette's movements to the point where they left the railroad track and took the driveway that led to West Logan. If they could only find out where the kids had gone after that last sighting, they told Judy, they might be able to get the investigation going again.

Judy matter-of-factly delivered a stunning piece of news.

"Well," she said, "they was at my house."

The gravity of the moment didn't register on Judy, but Robinson and Powers knew instantly they'd made a major breakthrough. "We'd been messin' with that case for twenty-five years, but we never knew where those kids went, until then," Robinson said.

For another two hours, they talked with Judy. She told them why Todd and Annette had come to the house, who was there at the time, and who walked away with the couple minutes before they were murdered.

The dam of lies, gossip, and forensic fairy tales that had held together for a quarter of a century started to crack, and the truth was finally flowing.

Powers and Robinson did not know it just then, but another major break in the case was occurring in a state prison eighty miles away.

Chester McKnight saw the light. Something he'd heard in a chapel service at the Marion Correctional Institution in London, Ohio, inspired him to approach Patrick Fisher, the state investigator stationed at the medium-security facility in the western Ohio flatlands. This was in the summer of 2006. McKnight was in jail for crimes that suggested his nickname, Chester the Molester, was well deserved. He had pleaded no contest to charges he'd set up a rendezvous for sex with someone in Cincinnati he thought was a sixteen-year-old girl. Instead, the "girl" he'd met in an online chat room turned out to be a Hamilton County sheriff's deputy. McKnight's sentence got booted up from eighteen months to eleven years after investigators found he'd downloaded a trove of child pornography onto his mother's computer. Whenever he got out of prison, Chester knew that he'd carry the repellent brand name of "registered sex offender."

Chester knew he couldn't go home again. This was his third go-round in the Ohio prison system. He'd served two previous terms for assaults on young women walking alone on railroad tracks in a town less than twenty miles from Logan. After his most recent conviction, his mother's neighbors had informed her that Chester would no longer be welcome in their trailer park.

After that, Chester started working toward ensuring that the state of Ohio would shelter him for the rest of his days. When he first approached Fisher, he said he had important information regarding an unsolved murder in Athens County, Ohio. By the time the information reached Athens County Sheriff Vern Castle, there was an expectation that McKnight was ready to confess to stabbing an Athens flower shop owner to death in the men's room of a state park.

Excited at the prospect of clearing a brutal murder case, Castle reported the news to the county's prosecuting attorney, David Warren. The prosecutor was pleased, but he suggested Castle do some checking before filing any charges. Pinning this killing on Chester proved problematic in the extreme—McKnight had been in prison at the time of that particular murder.

Later, McKnight told Fisher he wanted to confess to a double homicide in Logan that had occurred about twenty-five years earlier. An investigator from Hocking County came to the prison to interview McKnight. The investigator reported that Chester stated he had killed Todd and Annette, in return for a $5,000 payment from Dale Johnston. McKnight would later claim the investigator had coached him into implicating Johnston, and that claim would be supported by the results of a state-administered polygraph examination. When the Hocking County investigator asked McKnight to take a polygraph test, however, McKnight refused. The investigator went home, believing the trip had been a waste of time.

McKnight's statement might have been forgotten, except that his naming of Kenny Linscott as an accomplice was a potential link to the investigative lead that had been turned up by Robinson and Powers back in Hocking County. The two had reported their finding to local authorities, and then both ends of the case were referred to a squad of cold-case specialists working within the office of the Ohio attorney general.

In late 2006, Robinson and Powers met with Hocking County Prosecuting Attorney Larry Beal and Ed Kallay, an investigator for the cold-case squad. Beal said he would officially reopen the investigation into the 1982 murders, due primarily to the evidence that indicated Kenny Linscott may have been involved. A few days later, Powers and Robinson were informed that the investigation would be taken over by the Hocking County Sheriff's Office working jointly with the attorney general's investigators. They were allowed to chase down some leads on the Tex Meyers angle, but, essentially, they were off the case.

Judy Linscott was interviewed by the new team of investigators about the events of October 4, 1982. Todd and Annette had come to her house, she told them, and left about a half hour later with Kenny and another man she didn't know too well. She said he was short and a bit fat, and wore his hair bushy in the front and long in the back. This guy sort of reminded her of a chipmunk, she said. She was shown a photo array and was able to identify the man she'd seen walking away with Kenny, Todd, and Annette. The man she picked was Chester McKnight.

Back in prison, McKnight added to the momentum of the investigation. In the summer of 2007, McKnight had approached Patrick Fisher again, saying he was finally ready to talk truthfully about the murders of Todd and Annette. Fisher said McKnight seemed different this time. "He looked like the weight of the world had been lifted from his shoulders," Fisher said.

Kallay was part of the delegation of investigators who reinterviewed McKnight. He observed something happening to McKnight that, to him, resembled an internal struggle to tell the truth. McKnight started off by claiming again that Dale Johnston had hired him to do the killings, but the words started to stick in his mouth, Kallay said.

"He wanted to say more, but he didn't know how to do it," Kallay said. Then, McKnight started telling the story again, this time with both relief and an air of genuineness, Kallay said. McKnight said he'd done the shootings, and Linscott had helped to cut up the corpses. His prior statements that he was Johnston's paid hit man were lies, he admitted. He also agreed to submit to a polygraph examination. "You could tell it was bothering him, and he wanted to get it off his chest," Kallay said.

At first, McKnight told the investigators that he wanted the death penalty for his crimes. Later, he scaled back, requesting that the death penalty be taken off the table, in return for his cooperation. McKnight had only one other condition for the investigators. "His only concern then was that he'd be able to stay here. He wanted to do his time in Madison," Fisher said.

The investigators were not about to take Chester at his word. "That type of individual is the kind who's never been honest about anything, so we had to verify everything," said Matt Speckman, then the Hocking County sheriff's chief deputy, who became the lead local investigator for the reopened case. His partner was Logan PD Lt. Gregg Cluley.

In May 2008, McKnight was brought back to Logan, the first of three times he would walk the investigators through the crime scene. He showed them where the shootings had occurred, where the corpses had been dismembered, and where the torsos had been thrown into the river. Speckman said the investigators tested Chester's knowledge of the crimes. "We tried to goof him up," he said, by suggesting details they knew to be inaccurate. Each time Chester corrected them and kept his story in line with the known evidence.

Kallay said Chester convinced him as well. "Everything just fit together this time around," he said.

For further confirmation, Chester submitted to a lie-detector test, administered by Cynthia Erwin, a state polygraph expert. The following are some of the questions and McKnight's answers:

Q. Did you shoot Todd Schultz?

A. Yes.

Q. Did you shoot him in the cornfield we walked today?

A. Uh-huh.

Q. Did you have any part in dismembering his body and throwing his torso in the river?

A. Yes.

Q. Did you knowingly shoot Annette Johnston?

A. I don't remember. I ain't sayin' no.

Q. Was she present when you shot and killed Todd Schultz?

A. (nods in agreement)

Q. Did she say anything?

A. I can't recall. She was screaming.

Q. Was Kenny Linscott with you in the cornfield when you shot and killed Todd Schultz?

A. Yes.

Q. Did he help you cut up those bodies and dispose of their torsos in the river?

A. Yes.

Q. Did you help bury any of the body parts in the field?

A. No.

Q. Did you discard the gun anywhere?

A. No.

Q. Did Dale Johnston offer you $5,000 to kill those kids?

A. No.

Q. Did you have it in your mind to force her into some kind of sexual act, and that's why you had the gun?

A. Yes.

Speckman was new to the case, since he hadn't been a Hocking County sheriff's deputy when the killings occurred. So, he had no past performance on the case to defend. When he started to review the old case files, he was taken aback by the way they had been allowed to deteriorate. Much of the documentation and physical evidence had been stored in a building that had developed a leaky roof. Some of the evidence had suffered water damage, and some evidence was missing. "It was difficult to match up some of the evidence," he said. "We had to stay mostly with the new stuff."

Even so, Speckman was able to spot a major flaw in the prosecutors' original scenario of the crimes, especially the part where Johnston was supposed to have shuttled from Logan to his trailer and then back to town again. "That made no sense to me," he said. "If I lived out on Trowbridge Road and did the killings out there, why would I cut up the bodies and bring them back to a populated area to bury them?" he said.

There was, however, a gold nugget in the slag heap of old documents. Speckman and Cluley found the dispatcher's log that included a notation of a call from Kenny Linscott, inquiring about whether the bodies had been found. Speckman immediately saw the significance of the date of the call, the day before the discovery of the torsos in the river.

"That sold it to me," Speckman said. At that point, he said, he became convinced that "he [Linscott] knows what happened."

Speckman conducted and taped his first interview with Linscott in late 2007. At this point, Linscott was seriously ill, with heart and colon problems. Speckman told Linscott that he did not believe Dale Johnston had committed the murders. Linscott seemed to agree, saying, "I never did believe he did it."

If it wasn't Johnston, then who was it? Speckman told Linscott that there was credible evidence that Todd and Annette had come to Linscott's home just before they disappeared. At first, Linscott said he couldn't be sure about that. Then, he said maybe they were there, and maybe they weren't. Linscott described Todd as a friend who would come over to his house every now and then.

Linscott said he'd been drinking all day on the day of the murders. He said he went out barhopping with a friend that night. Speckman then told Linscott that he was fairly certain Todd and Annette had come to Linscott's house, because Judy Linscott remembered them coming over that day. Linscott responded, "Like I said, we may have talked." However, Linscott denied taking any part in the killings or the dismemberments.

When Speckman asked Linscott to explain his call to the sheriff's office, Linscott could offer none. At this point, Linscott abruptly ended the interview, saying talking about the murders "blew him away." "When we got to the punch line, he flipped," Speckman said.

From that point on, Speckman said, there was "absolutely no doubt in my mind" that Linscott had been a participant in the crimes. However, he added, he was also convinced that Linscott was just along for the ride in the death car McKnight was driving. "Kenny did not know those kids were going to die," Speckman said. He'd joined the group for what he thought would be a pot party that would lead to sex, but at this party, "Things went bad very fast," Speckman said. In 2011, Speckman moved to a position with the Ohio Bureau of Criminal Investigation.

The investigators had their case essentially wrapped up. Chester had confessed, and they wanted Kenny to do the same. Speckman and Kallay went to Linscott's home in late July, showed him a picture of McKnight, and asked him if he knew Chester. At first he said he didn't recognize him, but Linscott later conceded that the picture might be of a guy he'd met a few times. He said he didn't know the guy's real name, but people called him Chester the Molester. Linscott said he might have seen him a few times hanging out at the apartment complex they called the Animal House. Linscott said he went there to hang out and smoke dope; Chester was "someone you just tolerated." Speckman asked Linscott to continue the interview at the sheriff's office, and Linscott agreed.

Kallay did not bring it up during this interview, but he had developed information that led him to believe that Linscott and McKnight were more than casual acquaintances. "There was a whole group of people involved in a burglary ring," Kallay said. "That's how Kenny knew Chester."

Later that morning at the sheriff's office, Linscott admitted to the investigators that he dealt marijuana from his house, and Todd had been one of his steady customers. Then, the investigators showed Linscott parts of their videotaped interview with McKnight, particularly the part where Chester stated he'd connected with Todd and Annette at Linscott's house. When asked again whether Chester had been at his house that day, Linscott replied, "Maybe he was."

After he watched McKnight saying he'd used Linscott's gun to shoot Todd and Annette, Linscott did not deny it. Talk of the gun led Linscott into a discussion of his many suicide attempts. In one of those, Linscott went to the spot on the riverbank where the torsos of Todd and Annette had been thrown into the Hocking River, and he shot himself—in the shoulder. Linscott said he was "tired of life." When the questioners tried to get him to explain how his gun came to be Chester's murder weapon, Linscott said he was having trouble remembering details. He refined that statement, saying he couldn't remember "at this time."

They told Linscott that McKnight had treated the whole matter like a joke while he was making his statement. "It wasn't a joke," Linscott responded. He wasn't laughing, but he was teasing his interrogators. He put a percentage on how sure he was that he had been with Chester in the cornfield that day, but he also kept changing it. First, he was 20 percent sure, then it was 50 percent. By the time the interview was nearly over, about three hours after it had begun, Linscott had upped his degree of certainty to 90 percent.

After a break in the interview, Linscott admitted that he knew Chester better than he had let on before. He estimated that he'd "run around" with Chester ten times or more, and that Chester had been to his house at least twice. Linscott said he needed another break, to drain his colostomy bag.

Speckman challenged the alibi Linscott said he had given to police after the murders, asserting that Linscott had lied when he'd said he'd gone out barhopping that night. Linscott didn't deny Speckman's challenge. Then, Speckman asked him directly if he'd been with Chester and Todd and Annette that night. Linscott said that was possible. Speckman posed the same question again, asking for a yes-or-no answer. Instead, Linscott paused for a time and then sent out a clear signal that he was ready to make a deal. "So if I help you guys, what happens to me?" Linscott said.

At this point, Prosecuting Attorney Larry Beal was called into the room, and Linscott was informed of his rights. "Well, I could've been with them that night," Linscott said. He pegged his certainly level at 90 percent, but he wasn't quite ready to make an official statement. He said he needed more time "to study on it." The police made another appointment with Linscott for the following week, and then gave him a ride home.

When Speckman and Kallay went to Linscott's home to pick him up for the follow-up interview, Linscott begged off. He said a doctor had ordered him to stay home because he'd been passing blood into his colostomy bag. Besides, Linscott said, he wanted a lawyer. Linscott complied with the officers' warrant for a DNA sample and assured them he'd come down to the police station a few days later.

The appointed day came, but Linscott did not. Speckman went to Linscott's home, where Linscott showed Speckman a list of questions that Speckman had left with him earlier. To questions about his being with McKnight and Todd and Annette and about his gun being used in the shootings, Linscott had marked his answer as no. Speckman said he'd accept the questionnaire if Linscott had been truthful in his answers. If they were not truthful, Linscott should not give him the form, Speckman said. Linscott folded the paper and put it in his pocket. Speckman told Linscott the case against him would soon go to a grand jury.

In September 2008, McKnight and Linscott were both charged with murder in the deaths of Todd Schultz and Annette Johnston. Both men entered pleas of not guilty. Apparently, no one associated with this milestone thought or cared enough to give a heads-up to the man who'd been ticketed for execution for the same crimes. The only way Dale Johnston learned of his impending vindication was from a reporter calling him for comment. He told the reporter, "I've been praying for this day for twenty-seven years."

At first, McKnight's attorneys deluged the court with motions on their client's behalf, but McKnight's desire to admit his guilt prevailed. On December 18, at a hastily called hearing in the same courthouse where Johnston's conviction had been cheered so lustily, McKnight entered a plea of guilty and was sentenced to two twenty-year prison terms, to be served concurrently. He spoke very briefly, apologizing to the families but offering no explanation of why he had killed the young couple. He was not required by the court to offer any details of the crimes. He did, however, gallantly claim that he was responsible for "about 95 percent of the crime." He offered no insights into the 5 percent of the crime that his accomplice Kenny Linscott had committed, remarking only that Linscott "is on his deathbed anyway."

McKnight remained expressionless through much of the part of the proceeding where the victims' relatives are allowed to speak. But when Todd's younger sister Kendra held up a photograph of Todd's headstone, Chester wept.

The case against Kenny Linscott was not to be wrapped up so tidily. His court-appointed attorney, Bob Toy, a former prosecutor from Athens County, saw an opportunity to defend his client by using the threat of courtroom chaos. Chester McKnight's credibility was an easy target for Toy. Chester had apparently offered a false confession to another murder, and Toy would argue McKnight was doing the same this time. "Chester is making things up," Toy said. Also, Chester had changed his story since he first confessed to the Logan murders. McKnight had given interviews in prison during which he had claimed to have done everything himself and that Linscott wasn't involved. Who knew what Chester might say, if he were called to the stand at Linscott's trial?

Toy dismissed the lie-detector test that McKnight had passed. It couldn't be introduced as evidence against Linscott, and a seasoned convict like McKnight knew how to beat the machine, anyway. "I could get Chester to confess to killing the Czar of Russia, and I guarantee he'd be able to pass the lie-detector test," Toy said.

Toy put the prosecution on notice that he fully intended to put Dale Johnston on trial again. All the evidence used to obtain Johnston's conviction could be dredged up and trotted into court this time around, to be presented as Linscott's alternative theory of the crime. The courtroom would fairly ooze reasonable doubt.

The jury would never get to hear Judy Linscott testify that she saw Kenny walk off with the murder victims just before their deaths, Toy claimed. Even though the Linscotts were separated, they were still legally married, and Toy would make every effort to use the spousal privilege to keep her from taking the stand.

No wonder, then, that Kenny got the deal of the millennium. At another hastily called hearing in June 2009, the charges against Linscott were reduced from murder to a misdemeanor, gross abuse of a corpse. In return for his guilty plea, Judge Thomas Gerken, the brother of former prosecutor Charles Gerken, sentenced Linscott to the time he'd already served in jail, about ten months. The trial that no one seemed to want would never happen.

"Could I have proved his guilt to a jury? I don't know," said Laina Fetherolf, who had taken over as Hocking County prosecuting attorney at the beginning of the year. "I came in on the end of the thing," said Fetherolf, who was one year old when Todd and Annette were murdered.

In explaining why she reduced the charges so dramatically, Fetherolf cited McKnight's easily attacked credibility, plus the facts that some witnesses had died and some evidence had been lost.

She didn't need to mention how awkward it would have been for her, as the state's prosecutor of Linscott, to have to try to tear down in court all the evidence against Johnston that her predecessors had so painstakingly built up as fact.

The state's acceptance of guilty pleas from McKnight and Linscott, Fetherolf acknowledged, amounted to a repudiation of the findings of the original investigation. She said it now appears possible that the police in the 1980s "were not as thorough as they should've been," adding that she did not mean to extend that criticism to the prosecutors who tried the case against Johnston. "Generally, we prosecutors have to go with what the law enforcement officers bring us," she said.

Still, people in Logan wanted to know just what had happened in that cornfield. The first time around, they'd gotten nearly three weeks of courtroom theater, though most of it was fantasy. This show looked like it was going to close a half hour after it opened. Will Kernan, the friend of the Schultz family and the attorney whom Todd had consulted on the day he died, pressed the judge to order Linscott to testify about his participation in the crimes. He and others in the community questioned "whether the circumstances have been revealed adequately," he said. "I think, to put the family's minds to rest, and to put the minds of the community at large to rest, having the defendant state what exactly his role was in these events would be a great benefit."

Judge Gerken did allow Linscott the opportunity to speak—but in the next breath, he warned him against taking it. "In describing what you did in the murders, you subject yourself to civil liability, although you don't own anything," Gerken said, as reported in the *Logan Daily News*.

Kenny kept his mouth shut. A few minutes later, he walked out of the Hocking County Courthouse a free man. The state of Ohio could not impose any further punishment on him in connection with the murders of Todd and Annette. The case was closed . . . permanently.

Judge Thomas Gerken said in a 2011 interview with the author that he did not have the authority to compel Linscott to testify about the details of the crime. His advice to Linscott regarding possible civil liabilities was the type of admonition he routinely issues to criminal defendants at such hearings, he said.

As soon as he was freed, Linscott started talking—and what he said was that his guilty plea had been a sham. He only pleaded guilty to get his get-out-of-jail free card. He'd been framed, he claimed. He never knew Chester McKnight, and he was really innocent, just like that other guy who'd gotten convicted way back when.

—9—

CHESTER AND KENNY

The screaming boy wasn't just throwing a tantrum; he was publicly humiliating his mother. As the mother dragged him out of a downtown Nelsonville store and out into the town square, the eleven-year-old spewed profanity and curses at her. Allen Mohney recognized the two as his neighbors, Donna McKnight and her son Chester. He was a few years older than Chester, whom he knew as the kid nobody wanted to play with. Still, forty years later, he can still recall how difficult it was to watch the ugly scene. "He was being very vulgar to his mother," Mohney said.

Mohney was buddies with Chester's older brother, but he and most of the other kids avoided Chester whenever possible. "We just didn't want to be around him," Mohney said. Chester was a reclusive, moody kid with a volcanic temper and a foul mouth, he said. Chester had a nickname, though Mohney can't remember where it came from. "People have called him Chester the Molester for as long as I can remember," he said.

To Donna McKnight Ellinger, Chester, the younger of her two sons, was a mostly gloomy child, who seemed to have a knack for making the worst of just about any situation. "He was a kid that trouble just followed," she said.

Chester's father bolted the family when Chester was an infant, she said. The father was basically a deadbeat and a heavy drinker who never contributed to the upbringing of the children he abandoned, she said.

When Chester was still a boy, the family moved from Buchtel, a small mining community where the mines had long been shut down, into the nearby city of Nelsonville, about fifteen miles southeast of Logan. Lorena Harkless, who grew up in the same Nelsonville neighborhood, remembers Chester as more goofy than moody. There was a large grapevine in her family's yard where the kids used to like to swing and climb. Once, Chester fell off the vine and hurt himself. Harkless said her father decided he'd better cut the vine down after the accident. "Chester was a short, fat, jolly boy," she said. "Maybe he was a little stupid, but he laughed a lot."

Donna McKnight Ellinger remarried, but that lasted only a few years. When he was a teenager, Chester came home one day and found his stepfather dead of natural causes. Once again, Donna had to be both parents, plus holding down different factory jobs that usually involved rotating shift work. As he grew older, she said, Chester showed less respect for her and for whatever she tried to say to him.

"When I tried to tell him the right thing to do, he didn't want to do it," she said. "He'd come in the front door and go right out the back."

Chester entered Nelsonville-York High School, where he cultivated a reputation as an outcast. He played no sports, joined no clubs, and had no girlfriends, his mother said. "He had one good friend, and that was it," she said. That friend was believed by other students to be gay, Mohney said. The friend moved away, and Chester became even more sullen and withdrawn. He dropped out of school. "I just got tired of it," was the only explanation Chester offered. His mother didn't understand it either; she said Chester's teachers never reported to her that he was a problem student.

Chester started drinking and lying about his drinking, she said. For example, he got arrested for underage drinking, and his excuse was that he was only going along with the teens doing the drinking to be their designated driver, she said.

Dropping out only worsened Chester's chronic laziness, according to Donna: "Usually, he'd just lay on the couch and watch TV. I couldn't ever get him to mow the damn lawn."

Drugs became increasingly important to him, she said; as his usage increased, so did his mood swings. Practically anything could trigger his outbursts, which typically included cursing, shrieking, and throwing objects around the house, she said. "He never did hit me," she claimed, implying that this evidence of restraint was somehow a mark in Chester's favor. Perhaps she also meant that Chester was smart enough to avoid crossing the line of physical violence with the only person who cared for him and sheltered him.

Stoned, however, Chester was often an easier person to deal with than when sober, she admitted: "When he was on drugs, he was a happy kid, but when he was off, he was a holy terror."

His mother never learned why people often called him Chester the Molester. "I don't know who he molested," she said. During his prison interviews with the author, Chester acknowledged the nickname, but he claimed not to know where it came from, either.

To his mother, Chester's emotional problems didn't seem too far removed from the types of struggles most people have to deal with. "His nerves wasn't all that good," she said.

According to Chester, much of his youth wasn't all that good.

He spent his early years in his grandparents' home, where his mother moved with her children after Chester's father left. They moved in with one of his uncles after his grandparents died. Chester said he became "best of friends" with his uncle because "he kind of understood me. I was not like my brother; I just wanted to be left alone. My uncle told me he always wanted to be alone," McKnight said.

When he was still an adolescent, Chester said, his uncle introduced him to alcohol. "I loved it from the first drink," Chester said.

He had other male relatives that he did not like, he said. A different uncle who often babysat for him while his mother worked the late shift at the tire plant once started a fire in the woods and successfully blamed it on Chester, who received a beating for the incident, Chester said. Another uncle repeatedly told him he'd never amount to anything, Chester said.

The one relative he recalls with any fondness, the uncle who took him in, died when Chester was about thirteen. "I felt like my whole word fell apart, because he was the only one who understood me," Chester said.

When he was about twelve, Chester's mother remarried, bringing the family some financial stability. Having a stepfather did not mean an increase in structure or discipline in his life, Chester said. Rather, he had more freedom, which he would often use to hang out with older males who could buy liquor and beer for him. About six years later, he was home alone with his stepfather when the elder man died suddenly.

High school was never Chester's favorite place. He didn't make it past the second year. He had only one real friend at that time, an older fellow outcast he referred to as Cody. "We was always together, and we only trusted each other," Chester said. They even dropped out of school on the same day and went off together on a three-day drinking binge, Chester said.

Cody frequently carried a sawed-off shotgun, which impressed Chester. They'd drive around and shoot at road signs or go off into the woods and find something to shoot.

One evening in the woods, Chester and Cody were high and admiring the sunset. "We was telling each other how great the sunset was, and then Cody looked at me and told me goodbye," Chester said. "I asked him where he was going, and then I heard the blast from the shotgun. Blood was everywhere. I was stained with blood and other stuff," he said.

Chester said he ran off and found a pay phone, where he made an anonymous call to the police to report the death of his friend. Next, he went to Cody's parents to tell them what had happened. "They was shocked, but they kind of expected it," he said. Cody, he found out, was suffering from a very painful brain tumor. McKnight asked that Cody's real name not be used in this book.

Only once during his troubled life did McKnight seek professional help. While he was still a teenager, he said he suffered a "nervous breakdown." He spent "ninety days or so" at the Athens Mental Health Center, but he said he gained no insight into his problems. "They just gave me some drugs and shut me in a corner, like most of them do," McKnight said.

Sometime in 1979 or 1980, Chester and his mother moved to the Logan Arms Apartments so that Donna could be closer to her job at a tire plant. Several times during his interviews with the author, Chester referred to the place as the Animal House, as if to boast that he'd finally gained membership in the party crowd. "This was where I met Kenny Linscott, and so we became friends," McKnight said.

The move to Logan didn't bring about any improvement in the way Chester treated his mother. Rusty Spence, who also lived at the Logan Arms at the time, recalled Chester was "real mean to her. He'd say, 'Give me some money,' and she'd give it," Spence said.

Chester said his life in Logan was pretty much a quest to get high and stay high. He worked sporadically as a gas station attendant and a farmhand, he said. To supplement his income, he also "stole stuff," he said. "I was involved in a four-county theft ring that involved the Warren boys," McKnight said. (The Warren boys were leaders of an organized crime ring that will be discussed in a later chapter.)

Being part of the local drug and crime scene did not mean Chester gained any real friends. He didn't hang out at bars, and he didn't date, he said. His favorite thing to do was to go down to the river by himself to fish, drink, or do drugs. "I wasn't much of a people person," he said, without apparently appreciating the level of understatement in that remark. His life in the Logan years consisted mainly of "drinkin', druggin', and driftin'," he said.

McKnight did, however, manage to find a little time for romance.

Among his neighbors was a couple with three daughters. The girls seemed to Chester to be neglected by their father. One day, the girls were outside and invited Chester to play a game with them. He accepted, and afterwards, the mother invited him to their home for an introductory meeting. They became friends. Their relationship grew to the point where one of the girls felt comfortable enough to ask Chester to help her with her homework. "I told her that I would help her, and you wouldn't believe the smile I got out of her," McKnight said.

The woman had a sister, Diana, and she introduced her to Chester when they visited. Chester was attracted to Diana, but he really loved her two-year-old son Bobby. About a month after they met, Chester and Diana were married. Records in Hocking County show the marriage took place in early September, 1982—less than a month before the murders.

"I had a family that made me very happy," McKnight said. "It was like a dream."

To try to make the dream last, Chester promised to stop drinking and doing drugs. When Diana and her sister wanted to go out, Chester would volunteer to babysit for all their children.

"Bobby was my son, for we done everything together," McKnight said. "He made me feel great, like my life was worth living, especially when he would come running to me with his little arms out wide, yelling 'daddy!' Sometimes, I would pay more attention to him than I would her."

The couple and Diana's son moved into an apartment in the same complex. Their lease was a month-to-month proposition; their marriage was an even shorter-term deal.

McKnight's wife Diana, who asked that her current last name not be used, said her initial assessment of Chester was that "he was just a sweet guy, good to me and my son." Chester formed a strong bond with her little boy, she said. "He loved my son, and my son loved him to death," she said, during a 2011 interview.

For Chester and Diana, domestic tranquility lasted only a few weeks. "We started arguing about everything," Diana said. She was most deeply upset by Chester's persistent drug use and heavy drinking, she said.

"I didn't need that," she said. She took her son and left, going back to her family in a neighboring county.

Diana said she never knew anything about the 1982 murders in Logan, or about Chester's confession to the crimes, until the author told her during their telephone interview. She did say, however, that she never saw anything to indicate Chester was capable of the kind of violence that befell Todd and Annette. "It's hard to believe," Diana said.

"They had a flaky marriage," said Chester's mother. She recalled Chester wanted to make her the little boy's guardian, but Diana wouldn't hear of it.

Diana also started directing her attentions elsewhere, McKnight said. She started going out more often and was obviously seeing other men, McKnight said.

Since the breakup, McKnight said, he has never seen Diana or her son again.

Once his vision of being a father and husband was shattered, McKnight said, he plunged even deeper into darkness. Besides the drinking and the drugs, he said he started showing a mean side, carrying a gun and a machete nearly all the time.

"I didn't care what happened, because I lost everything that I ever wanted in life," McKnight said. "Everybody knew I was on the highway to hell."

After the murders, McKnight said, it took him a couple of days to grasp the reality of what he had done. "I was too high to really comprehend at that time," he said. He said he went to hide out with some friends who lived a few counties away. But it was only a matter of months later that Chester was back, living with his mother, who'd returned to Nelsonville, a fifteen-minute drive from the cornfield.

"He would always come back," Donna said of Chester. But he seldom accounted for his comings and goings, she said. He would often lie about in the house during the day and then head out at night, she said.

Chester never acted like a fugitive, never showed any concern that the police would come knocking at his door. "I could've gotten away with it," he said. "I mean, nobody questioned me, no nothin'." At that time, in the early months of 1983, the investigation was at its peak, though the general public did not know that it was focused exclusively on Dale Johnston. When the police finally indicted Johnston in September of that year, Chester said his conscience wasn't troubled a bit. "Wasn't me," he said casually.

As the justice system closed in on the innocent man, the guilty man was prepping for a replay of the crime. He started hanging out on the river again, near the railroad trestle bridges. He became a sort of troll, lurking around the same set of railroad tracks and the same river—and it was all just a few miles downstream from Logan.

On November 3, 1983, Chester committed a crime with some striking similarities to what he'd done in Logan. The major difference this time was his failure to get his victim to the point where he could do what he did to Annette. He pulled a knife on a college coed who was walking the railroad tracks in Nelsonville. He pulled her down the railroad embankment, intending to rape her. However, the young woman was too quick for him. She escaped, identified him to police, and he was arrested.

McKnight pleaded guilty to a charge of abduction. In 1984, he was sentenced to three to fifteen years in prison. However, he qualified for "shock probation" and was released after serving six months of his sentence. His five-year term of parole was terminated less than two years later. His probation officer stated that Chester no longer needed supervision.

Less than five months later, though, the troll returned. On September 12, 1986, a nineteen-year-old female student at Hocking College in Nelsonville was doing what she and other students often did, taking a shortcut by walking the railroad tracks to the campus. She was in a hurry, on her way to a final exam.

She testified in a sentencing hearing that she passed a short man standing near the trestle bridge where the tracks go through a city park. She and the man exchanged a greeting, a brief hi, even though they didn't know each other. After she passed him, she started to walk faster, when she heard his footsteps behind her. Then she turned around.

"Say goodnight, baby," Chester McKnight said, as he swung a tire iron, striking the woman in the head. Her turnaround may have saved her. The blow stunned but did not incapacitate her. Chester grabbed her arm, but she was able to pull away and escape. She made it to a hospital, and she reported the assault to police.

Nothing happened in the investigation until about a week later, when the woman was on her way to the hospital for a follow-up treatment to her head wound. She spotted the man who'd attacked her, standing in an alleyway near the hospital. Chester was arrested and charged with felonious assault.

Chester at first told police he wanted to confess. He then changed his mind and entered a not-guilty plea, then changed it again and pleaded no contest. He told police he was unemployed and was receiving a monthly welfare payment of $134.

At his sentencing hearing, McKnight told the judge he didn't remember the assault. He claimed he had been under the influence of prescription drugs prescribed for him after he'd suffered a motorcycle accident.

"Well, your honor, I'm sorry this had to happen," McKnight said. "I just lost it. Which, you know, I'm drug-dependent anyway. Seems like I can't go a day without, you know, anything. I have blackouts, you know, when I get so high, things, you know, I just lose track."

McKnight stated he'd been taken to jail for public intoxication nearly every night during the previous month's Parade of the Hills Festival. "Every time they took me in, I was at, you know, I was always, uh, had a substance," he said.

Something else Chester said to the judge made the prosecuting attorney remember that brief hearing twenty-three years later. Bob Toy, who was Kenny Linscott's defense attorney in 2008–2009, was an assistant prosecutor in Athens County then, and he recalled McKnight asking the judge for the maximum penalty, even if it meant life in prison. If he were let out of prison, he'd probably commit the same type of crime, Toy said McKnight told the judge. McKnight claims he can't recall making such a statement.

The strange request may or may not have influenced the judge. Chester's past record of assault must have. He was sentenced to from six to fifteen years in prison, and he served twelve years in Madison, before being released on parole in 1999.

For the next few years, McKnight managed to keep his felony record clean. He even developed a relationship with a woman, Donna McKnight said, adding that his girlfriend died in 2009. By this time McKnight was in his forties, and his primary residence was still his mother's trailer.

Again, Chester's prison-free period outlasted his parole by only a short time. In 2002, Chester told his mother that he was taking his sister's car to go to apply for a job at a supermarket. That was a lie.

Instead, McKnight drove to Cincinnati, about 150 miles away, where he was arrested for the last time.

He pleaded guilty to a charge of gross sexual imposition involving a minor and was sentenced to eighteen months. Athens County officials assisted in the investigation by confiscating McKnight's mother's computer, which he had been using. They found a trove of child pornography, after which they filed new charges, which ultimately caused McKnight's prison sentence to be bumped up by thirteen years.

During the investigation of the sexual predator charge, McKnight's Nelsonville girlfriend filed a complaint alleging that McKnight took her adolescent daughter out for a drive in the country, pulled over, and fondled her. The alleged molestation had occurred three years earlier, when the girl was twelve, according to the complaint. McKnight was interviewed by Jim Thompson, who by then was a sheriff's deputy in Athens County assigned to Child Protective Services. Unlike the time more than twenty years earlier when Thompson neglected to make a recording of his interrogation of a double murder suspect, he taped his interview with McKnight. According to the transcript of that interview, the topic of the 1982 murders never came up.

McKnight's response to the latest charges: "It's a freakin' soap opera." He claimed his reputation as an unstable weirdo was due to vicious rumors. During the interview, McKnight supplied Thompson with some details of his background. He said he was receiving disability payments of about $115 per month, as well as food stamps amounting to about $125 per month. He also stated he dropped out of high school in Nelsonville but earned a GED in prison. The molestation charge was never prosecuted.

The sexual predator charges carried the additional penalty of mandatory registration as a sex offender. McKnight then realized that whenever he got out of prison, he couldn't go back to his mother again. That's when he started confessing to murders.

Donna McKnight said her son's confessions might have been his way of lining up lifetime accommodations. "Maybe he made it up to stay in prison," she said. There's another factor besides true contrition that could have factored into his thinking: life in prison is generally easier for a killer than for a child molester.

Chester's mother said she'd never suspected her son was involved in the Logan murders. "How in the world did he keep that a secret from me for twenty-six years?" she said.

McKnight had plenty of time to become comfortable with life behind bars. Of the twenty-seven years that passed between the murders of Todd and Annette and his guilty plea, he spent eighteen in prison.

"I guess this is the best place for me," McKnight said.

In contrast, Kenny Linscott has never seen the inside of a state prison. And now that he has been released and is seriously ill, chances are he never will. Some people who knew him well, however, say he's done things that could well have earned him serious jail time.

"The twenty-seven years I was with him, he did some funky stuff," said Linscott's estranged wife Judy.

In one of his funkier episodes, Kenny apparently tried to kill himself and his whole family, she said. "He set the garage on fire, then came to bed and passed out," she said. A neighbor who saw someone setting the fire woke the family up and called the fire department. Arson investigators labeled the fire "suspicious," but Kenny was never treated as a suspect by police. He was even able to collect an insurance settlement for the fire damage, she said. When she confronted Kenny with her suspicions that he was responsible, he told her, "Oh, I was just outside pissin'," she said.

That incident was one of a series of times when Judy Linscott stayed silent when she believed her husband had committed a serious crime. "He tried to burn the house down around us, and I never did anything about it," she said.

Another arson, which occurred not long before the murders of Todd and Annette, made Kenny something of a pariah in his own neighborhood.

Rusty Spence, who grew up as a neighbor of the Linscotts in West Logan, recalled Kenny having a fierce argument with a man who rented an apartment from Kenny's parents. After the argument, someone poured gas onto the tenant's Oldsmobile and set it afire. This was an obvious case of arson, but police did not investigate Kenny as a suspect, Spence said. "I used to run with Kenny a lot, but not after that," he said.

Judy Linscott said other neighbors started backing away from Kenny after the car-fire episode. "After people caught on to what he was doing, hardly anybody would associate with him," she said.

That didn't stop Kenny from gloating, she said. "He just sat back and laughed," she said. "He thinks if he does something and nobody sees him, he'll get away with it."

Kenny's confidence in his crime-skating skills must have risen after the murders of Todd and Annette. The young couple he walked away with had turned up missing. When Kenny did come home, he had a deep cut on his arm wrapped with a bloody rag. He said he'd put his hand through a window, but Judy knew that was a lie. There hadn't been any windows broken around the house that day.

When they went to the hospital to have the wound treated, the doctor said it looked to him as if Kenny had been cut with by a knife blade, Judy said.

Kenny also called the police to inquire about whether the bodies had been found—before anyone else knew there were even bodies to find.

On a night shortly after the disappearances, Rusty Spence walked the railroad tracks from West Logan into Logan. At the trestle bridge, he said a man crying uncontrollably. It was Kenny Linscott. When Spence asked him what was wrong, Kenny would only say, "You wouldn't understand."

Judy Linscott saw all that, and all her suspicions seemed to be confirmed when the bodies were discovered. "I just about lost it then," she said. But she didn't come forward, and the police never bothered to come to her. Part of her silence was due to her belief that no one would listen, she said. "I had suspicions, but if I'd said anything to his Mom and Dad, they'd have just taken his side," she said.

Judy was far from the only person in West Logan who suspected Kenny. When police started searching the cornfield area, Rusty Spence said, Kenny became visibly agitated. Kenny started running between the cornfield and the small group of West Logan residents who gathered outside as the news spread about the discoveries being made just across the railroad tracks, Spence said. "He'd run back and forth to tell us what was happening. He said they were finding body parts," Spence said. "I didn't see the law telling him stuff like that," he said.

Spence said his suspicions of Linscott were shared by many in West Logan. Matt Spence, Rusty's younger brother, said he was present when police canvassing the neighborhood interviewed his mother and father. "Dad said, 'That boy's the one who done it,'" Matt Spence said, adding that it was clear to everyone in the room that his father was referring to Kenny Linscott.

The crimes were the talk of West Logan, not to mention the state of Ohio. Every major newspaper and television station in the state covered the story and its impact on the small city. The residents of West Logan told each other about their interviews with the police. Rusty Spence estimated that dozens of people in the neighborhood gave Kenny's name to police as a possible suspect.

The news of the murder investigation stayed on the newspaper front pages and at the top of the television news shows for weeks. The unrelenting publicity disturbed Kenny, Judy Linscott said. "Anytime he saw it on the news, he'd get up and walk away," she said. Kenny became increasingly moody and, for a long time, he wouldn't go near the cornfield and the river where he used to spend hours practically every day, she said.

During the early stages of the investigation, the *Logan Daily News* printed an article that included references to an FBI profile of the killer. According to the profile, the killer was probably a loner who had a history of poor relationships with women. Rusty Spence read the article and believed the profile confirmed his suspicions of Linscott. He knew that even though Linscott had a live-in girlfriend, he spent many nights down by the river. Spence went into the sheriff's office to report his suspicions, but Ray Davis, the deputy he talked to, showed no interest in his information. "It was like he didn't care what I was saying," Spence said. Davis did not respond to the author's request for an interview.

As the case progressed to the indictment and convictions of Dale Johnston, Spence figured he must have been wrong about Linscott. More than twenty-five years later, though, a new set of investigators came to him with questions about Kenny Linscott and Tex Meyers, making it clear they had reopened the case and suspected those two men. This time, they were interested in what Spence told them, and this time, Spence would learn that his original suspicions had been right on target.

For Judy Linscott, things did not get much better for her or her four children in the years after Kenny got passed over as a suspect. "Kenny got worse," she said. "From the time he got up till he passed out, he'd be drinkin' and partyin'," she said. The couple got married in 1983, but there really was no honeymoon period, she said. "All the time, he'd beat on me. He'd beat me in front of the children."

Throughout those years, Kenny rarely worked, she said. The few times he took a job, he was fired shortly after starting, she said. She raised the children mostly on welfare payments and whatever Kenny's parents gave her, she said.

She stayed with him, and stayed silent about what she knew, partly from fear, she said. "I was afraid to leave," she said. "I knew what he was capable of doing. Many times, he'd tell me, if he couldn't have me, no one would."

By 2006, Judy had finally had enough. She left Kenny and started dealing with her own drug problems. When Jim Powers, the first law officer ever to interview her about the case, asked her what she knew, she told the truth—that her husband and the man she identified as Chester McKnight walked away from her house with Todd and Annette minutes before the murders were committed.

In court, Kenny Linscott's guilty plea became at least a partial confirmation of Judy's story. He offered no details, but his plea enabled him to leave jail that same day, after having spent ten months in custody for participating in crimes for which another man had been sentenced to death twenty-six years earlier. Back then, the people of Logan had cheered the guilty verdict, but at Linscott's sentencing hearing, a relative of Todd Schultz asked for calm. "I wouldn't want anyone in the community to be violent toward him," said Greg Schultz, Todd's older brother. "I would hope the people of Logan just avoid the guy."

That irony is lost on Linscott. He doesn't think he should have spent a single day in jail. In an August 2009 interview with the author, Linscott spoke with defiance, though he looked like a defeated man. He walks with a stoop and a shuffle. His bullet-shaped head has gone mostly bald. Linscott repudiated his guilty plea, adamantly denying that he'd had anything to do with the murders:

Q. On October 4, 1982, did Todd Schultz and Annette Johnston come to your house?

A. No.

Q. So, you don't know anything about the crimes that happened that day?

A. No.

Q. Did you know Chester McKnight at all?

A. No, never seen him till he was pointed out to me in court.

Q. So, there wasn't any connection between your arm injury and what happened on the riverbank?

A. No.

Q. Do you have any knowledge about whether those kids were around your house, in that neighborhood on that day?

A. Never had a clue.

Q. Did you ever sell dope?

A. Nope.

But if he never knew Chester, and Chester never knew him, why did Chester implicate him in the murders? Certainly, Chester couldn't have picked the name Kenny Linscott at random. Linscott's response to that query was to blame the police. "My name wasn't brought up till the cops brought it up," he said. Somehow, he said, the police must have fed his name to McKnight, to make McKnight's confession fit the evidence implicating Linscott that was being developed in the renewed Hocking County investigation. It was all put together in what Linscott called "a nice neat package."

But whatever happened to his alibi? If he had really been cleared in 1982, why didn't his alibi hold up in 2007? At first, Linscott claimed that people who could have supported his barhopping alibi had either died or moved away. Then he reverted to his claim that he's the victim. "I will always feel like I got framed, no gettin' around it," Linscott said.

Q. And now are we at the point where you're saying they fucked up again?

A. Yep. I believe in my heart that they screwed up again. I mean, I'll never be able to prove it, but in my heart, I do believe that.

Q. Because they'll never reopen this case now?

A. Right.

Toward the end of the interview, Linscott gave a couple of other puzzling answers. Regarding McKnight's confession, Linscott said, "Chester's admitted to crimes he couldn't possibly have done." How would Linscott be able to make a flat statement like that? He didn't elaborate, but how would he know Chester could not have committed the crimes, unless he also knew who did?

Linscott also claimed his life had been threatened. "I have a big target on my back," Linscott said. "A few people I know, they say if they catch me, I'm in trouble."

But why would Kenny's former friends want him dead? Could he implicate some of them for helping him bury the body parts? Or could he have been connected to some larger criminal enterprise whose members don't want him talking?

The years since the murders have not been kind to Kenny. "I've had two bypasses on my leg. I've had five heart attacks, triple bypass. I've got a pacemaker with a defibrillator built in. I've got first stage emphysema, and it's not gettin' any better," he said. Also, he can't get too far away from his colostomy bag. He's forty-eight, but looks more like sixty-eight.

Kenny doesn't want people to think of him as a butcher's assistant. He doesn't want anything but a little peace and quiet, he said. "I just want to be left alone," he said. "Let me go on and live my life."

In March 2010, Linscott met briefly with the author for a second time. He had moved from a halfway house to a three-room apartment in Logan. He said he had been hospitalized numerous times in the past few months, and he was faced with the prospect of more major heart surgery in the near future. It's an effort to move around, he said, with a look of overwhelming weariness in his red-rimmed eyes that had sunk deep into his skull. He is indigent, he said, subsisting on food stamps and government rent vouchers.

But, was he ready to tell what happened that night in 1982? "I'm stickin' with my story," he said.

−10−

BLOOD ON THE CORN

Twilight gave its first caress to the autumn sky, heralding the rise of the corn moon. It was October 4, 1982.

Todd and Annette walked up to Kenny's house for a beer and a toke. They didn't know their killer would soon crash the party.

Kenny and a few of his buddies were already way ahead of Todd and Annette. They'd been drinking and doing drugs most of the day, which is to say, they were having an ordinary day. "They were heavy into it," said Judy Linscott. The party place actually was Kenny's parents' home, a modular unit connected to three or four other homes facing an alley that connected the parallel streets of Homer and Charles in West Logan. Kenny had brought his sixteen-year-old girlfriend Judy there to live with him a few months earlier. There were open spaces on either side of the alley, some of which the neighbors used for gardens. Pedestrian traffic was often channeled through the alley, making the Linscott home a natural informal gathering place.

It was not random sociability that brought Todd and Annette up the alley. They wanted to score, and they knew Kenny's was the place to go. They weren't planning on staying long. Todd was supposed to pick up his little brother at soccer practice, and later he was supposed to go to a volunteer firefighters meeting with his father.

Todd wasn't looking for a big score. He couldn't afford it. He'd been scratching for money most of the day, talking with his father about getting a place where he and Annette could have some privacy and consulting with the family's neighbor and attorney about whether he could force Annette's parents to give her the little orange Buick Skyhawk they'd promised. So, he settled for a quarter-ounce bag of pot. He grabbed a beer, but Annette didn't want anything to drink.

Annette wasn't disposed to hang out for long. One of the guys at Linscott's was that creepy Tex Meyers, the one who worked at Animal Crackers and who had this fantasy that Annette was his girlfriend. She was with Todd, her real boyfriend and unofficial fiancé, but that didn't keep Tex from flirting with her.

Less than a half hour had passed before Todd and Annette were ready to leave. By that time, though, a short guy, maybe a few years older than Todd, had filtered into the group. He could have seen them walking the railroad tracks and followed them to Kenny's. They'd seen him around a few times, but they didn't really know him. That guy was Chester McKnight.

Even though Chester spent most of his time doing solitary things on the banks of the Hocking River, he liked to think of himself as a party animal. "It was a party," Chester said of the scene that day at Kenny's. "Every day was a party day." Chester had a pretty good idea there'd be a party going on at Kenny's. "I knew he got high, I knew he drank. Who didn't?" Chester said.

"It was kind of like me goin' over there to see what was goin' on, and there were a few people there, drinkin' and smoking, you know, so I just joined in also," Chester said. "I went in and started to party with 'em, and everything just started workin' out really well."

To Chester, the presence of Tex was spoiling the party atmosphere.

"I just finished my beer, and so I thought that I would go into the kitchen and fix me a double shot of Jack and a beer," Chester said. He saw Tex and Annette; they seemed to be arguing.

"He thought he had ties to Annette, but on the day it happened, he was over at Kenny's, and after awhile, I was watching him slither around like the bug that he was," McKnight said. When Tex looked at Annette, the lust was obvious, McKnight said. "I seen his eyes get that gleam in them, like he wanted to hurt her."

McKnight injected himself into the conversation, asking if there was a problem. McKnight suggested that Annette should leave, and she did. That angered Tex, who threatened Chester, saying McKnight would "pay for what he did."

Chester responded by pulling out his gun and jamming the barrel against Tex's head. "You want to see how this works?" he hissed into Tex's ear. Chester told Tex to get lost, and Tex obeyed.

Chester was just as hungry for Annette as Tex had been, but he hoped she would see his gunplay as an act of gallantry. "I was ready to put him down, because I was trying to impress her for taking up for her," he said.

As Todd and Annette started to leave, Chester said, "You want to party a little more?" Todd seemed agreeable, and Annette went along with her boyfriend. Chester invited Kenny to come along.

Kenny fell in with Chester, Todd, and Annette. As the group of four left Linscott's house, Kenny called back to Judy, "We're takin' off to get more beer." That was rather odd, Judy recalls thinking at the time. "I couldn't figure out why they were walkin' to get beer," she said. There wasn't anyplace to buy beer within walking distance, though there was a car sitting in the parking space that Kenny could have used, if he really wanted beer. But she had a new baby and Kenny's ailing mother to look after, so she shrugged and watched them walk away.

When Chester, Kenny, Todd, and Annette walked down the alley, across Homer Street and down the access road that led to the tracks, they were basically retracing the route Todd and Annette had taken to get to Kenny's house.

They stopped on the tracks to light up a joint, but Chester saw something that made him stop. "We was just goin' to party some more. I mean, you know, there was some people out in their backyards and stuff, and, you know, we just didn't, didn't want to be seen," he said.

Chester said he saw a woman and some kids. That was probably Shirley Frazier, the Lancaster woman who had come to her mother's house on Homer Street to pick up her children. She saw a young couple and an older man on the tracks. The man went down from the tracks and into the cornfield. The younger man followed next, she said. The girl stomped her foot in apparent frustration, but she followed the others down the opposite side of the embankment. Frazier's attention went back to her children.

Chester had beckoned Todd and Annette into the unplanted swale within the cornfield on the premise that they'd have more privacy to smoke their dope. The rows of closely planted cornstalks ready for harvest didn't look too inviting to Annette, but she overcame her reluctance and joined the others.

Chester tried to keep the party atmosphere going. "I was sittin' around, kind of teasin' Annette, how cute she was, and, uh, you know," he said. "After we all smoked a couple of joints, I asked Annette if maybe she was looking for some fun. When she said no, that is when I tried to make her feel guilty about me saving her from Tex," he said.

"We was just like talkin', jokin' around, and then the jokin' started gettin' serious, and that's when it started getting' more hectic," Chester said.

The "something" Chester said he had in mind was to "pull a train"—that is, to have group sex. Todd got angry at the little weasel who wanted to screw his girl, and he lunged at Chester. Todd, the goofy, likeable slacker acted heroically—but in that same instant, the party was over.

"I just said, 'To hell with it,'" Chester said. "I pulled out the gun, shot him, and she started screamin', and I shot her."

Back in her mother's yard, Shirley Frazier heard the shots, one burst of three followed seconds later by a girl's screams and then by a second burst of three more. A few minutes later, she saw the man she'd seen with the couple come back up to the tracks, look around, and then skulk away. Later, she repeatedly tried to report what she'd seen to the police, but they disregarded her, the only eyewitness to the prelude to the killings.

By this time, the killer had the cover of darkness. Chester and Kenny decided they couldn't leave the corpses where they were. Kenny went back to his house to get some tools. Then they dragged or carried the corpses through the cornfield from the killing spot to a rocky outcropping they knew on the banks of the river. They stripped the bodies and laid them out on the stone. Chester recalled the "rush" he got from seeing Annette's body. "It was really a waste of a good piece of meat," he said.

The decision to dismember the corpses was, on a surface level, a practical one. Chester said he thought it would make it more difficult to find the bodies. However, he also conceded there was something far darker at work inside him. "I didn't just kill them, but I took it to the steps of a madman. I butchered them," he said.

Kenny held the victims' limbs while Chester cut them off. They tossed the torsos into the river. There were more cutting wounds on Todd's body than on Annette's. Part of that was due to the difficulty in carving up a human being. "I was . . . just getting' tired," Chester said. However, he added, he was especially angry at Todd because if Todd had just been more accommodating, maybe they could have had some sex, and maybe nobody would've died. Chester inflicted a final indignity on his victims. He cut off Todd's penis and put it in Annette's mouth.

At that point, Chester was spent. "When it was over, it was over," he said. He left the area, with the couple's heads and limbs and clothing still on the banks of the river. He said he told Kenny to take care of the rest. He claims not to know how the body parts came to be buried back in the cornfield. Linscott did not come back home until at least three hours later. He had suffered a deep gash to his arm, and he had pressed a bloody piece of cloth to it, but the wound would require treatment at a hospital.

Chester said he still is unable to explain why the chance meeting with two people he barely knew disintegrated so rapidly into a savage double murder. When he speaks of it now, as a fifty-year-old prison inmate with a potbelly and a head sparsely covered with hair, he talks in a detached, matter-of-fact tone, as if he were analyzing a bad career move. "I've been thinking about that ever since it happened," he said. "Really, it was on a whim."

But where does that rage spring from? All through his life, his major traumas were mostly inflicted on him by men, yet he vented his frustrations and humiliations on women, even the ones who cared for him. Does he hate women?

"It's possible," Chester said. "You know, we can all speculate."

—11—

GUILTVILLE, USA

The evidence that Todd and Annette had been murdered in the cornfield was like a blimp floating over West Logan with a crawl sign flashing: "FIND KILLER HERE."

Two women sitting at a McDonald's drive-through heard the shots.

A security guard on another side of the cornfield heard the shots.

Shirley Frazier not only heard the shots, she saw a young couple following a man into the cornfield minutes before the shots were fired.

Several witnesses saw Todd and Annette walking toward West Logan on the tracks; one witness saw them taking the driveway that led into West Logan.

The night-shift worker walking the tracks to work heard strange noises coming from the cornfield and was so alarmed by them that he turned back, went home, and drove to work.

Janice Moyer saw a late-night caravan of vehicles going over the driveway and down toward the cornfield. She was concerned enough to wake up her husband.

Numerous West Logan residents told police that Kenny Linscott should be considered a suspect. One resident went to the sheriff to transmit his suspicions more emphatically.

Kenny Linscott himself made a suspicious phone call to police before the bodies were found.

Linscott was seen with his arm bandaged from a cut he suffered on the night of the murder, a cut that was treated at a local hospital.

None of that evidence came as hindsight. All of it was given to police in the early days of the investigation—and all of it was ignored or discarded. Some of these witnesses who came forward were treated like fools or nuisances by the police.

Why? That question arose as soon as the case was reopened in 2007.

"It [evidence that the killings had occurred in the cornfield] was standing there right in front of them," said Hocking County Chief Deputy Matt Speckman, who reviewed the original case files twenty-five years after the murders. To him, it made "no sense" for the investigators in the 1980s to pursue a highly convoluted scenario of the crimes when the answers were to be found where Todd and Annette's bodies had been found.

The Logan Police Department officer who led the first investigation, Jim Thompson, did not respond to requests for interviews for this book.

The silence only ramps up the volume of the questions. Why would experienced police investigators work so hard to avoid looking in the obvious direction? Why didn't any of the investigators follow up on the numerous tips that Kenny Linscott was probably involved? Linscott never left the neighborhood, but according to his own account, no police officers ever came to him with questions. And, he said, after he went into the sheriff's office and made a statement with a flimsy alibi, the statement was either never entered into the case files or was deliberately tossed away.

Judy Linscott was right there in Kenny's house in West Logan from the very beginning of the case. No one from the police interviewed her. After the murders, she was still only Kenny's girlfriend, not his wife. Perhaps she was afraid of him even then, but it seems reasonable to believe she might very well have told the truth—if anyone had bothered to ask. When she was finally asked, twenty-five years later, if she'd seen Todd and Annette that day, she responded affirmatively and truthfully. Her answer broke the case in 2007, and it could easily have done the same in 1982.

Sheriff Jones personally intervened to cut off the investigation of Tex Meyers's possible connection to the crimes. Jones's reason: he assumed Kevin "Tex" Meyers was the same person as a local named Kevin Meyers who came from "a good family," and so he did not think the lead was worth pursuing. As it turned out, two witnesses have now stated that Tex Meyers was at Linscott's house when Todd and Annette arrived. Meyers was described as nervous and fearful after a brief interview with the police, but he offered to come in for further interrogation. Had Meyers been questioned thoroughly, he could certainly have led the investigators to Kenny Linscott and perhaps Chester McKnight.

Clearly though, Chester and Kenny had no political power or direct connections to local authorities. They were trolls, deadbeats, druggies. They could not, on their own, have deflected the investigation away from them and onto Dale Johnston.

Perhaps one reason the police did not treat Kenny Linscott as a suspect is that they were paying him. When asked by the author during a January 2012 phone conversation whether he had functioned as a confidential informant for the Hocking County Sheriff's Office, Linscott replied, "At one time or another, I was." He declined to provide details on the nature of his informant activities. He did, however, note that he did not work directly with Sheriff Jimmy Jones. Linscott also said he did not know whether Tex Meyers had ever been a police informant.

Jones said he was unaware of the informant status of either Linscott or Meyers. However, during a January 2012 phone conversation he added that either man could have worked for one of his deputies without Jones's knowledge.

And what of the criminals they may have been associated with? Some of the key detectives in the reopened investigation, including Ed Kallay, Jim Powers, and Rodney Robinson, developed evidence that indicated that McKnight and Linscott were both low-level operatives in an organized burglary ring. Chester admitted his involvement in the ring. He also told Ed Kallay that he and Linscott had committed an unspecified number of residential burglaries together, working for a crime ring called the "Warren Gang" (pronounced *Ware*-en in Central Ohio). McKnight said he was, and is, fearful of retaliation from the Warrens.

He has good reason to be afraid. The Warrens were a powerful gang that operated virtually unchecked throughout nearly twenty counties of southeastern Ohio for decades. Their primary business was robbing homes; and they specialized in stealing guns, safes, and antiques, according to Bob Smith, who, as an Ohio assistant attorney general, led the Ohio Organized Crime Commission that investigated and successfully prosecuted the gang leaders in the late 1980s and early 1990s.

In the gang's heyday, it was responsible for thousands of burglaries, Smith said. Most of the time, they'd break in when no one was home, but one branch of the gang grew bold enough to break in whether or not the house was empty and then tie up anyone who happened to be home while they ransacked the place, he said.

Two brothers, John and Paul Warren, were the main gang leaders, along with their partner Tom Cummings. John was the more outgoing brother, Smith said, while Paul was more reticent. Cummings was functionally illiterate, to the point where his wife had to read restaurant menus for him, but he was an expert in evaluating antiques.

Smith said the gang developed a technique in which they posed as small-time antique dealers operating mostly out of flea markets. At the flea markets, they'd scout for potential targets by striking up conversations with the passing customers. In particular, they targeted elderly people, who were more likely to have valuable antiques. They'd find a mark, learn something about their vehicle, then go out to the parking lot to get the license number. In those days, it was easy to find people's home addresses if you had their license plate numbers, Smith said. Then, the gang would stake out the home, or, if the targets had been kind enough to provide their vacation plans, they'd break in at their leisure and clean the place out. They would fence the stolen goods through an operative in West Logan. As their volume of stolen goods increased, they'd take truckloads of loot to the South for resale, ranging as far as Georgia and Florida. When the gang was finally stopped, investigators found one of their warehouses, near Atlanta, stocked with more than $1 million in stolen antiques, Smith said.

One of the major investigative sources was a gang member turned informant named Fred Woyan. Smith said Woyan possessed a near-photographic memory and was able to take investigators to hundreds of homes that had been burglarized by the gang.

Rodney Robinson, also a member of the gang task force, interviewed Woyan several times. Woyan gave him details of Kenny Linscott's dealings with the gang. He described Linscott as a fringe member of the gang, who would come to the gang's favored bar, the First Chance-Last Chance, and pass along tips regarding potential burglary targets. One of the people Linscott served up to the gang was his own sister, Robinson said Woyan told him. Linscott's sister was the widow of a state trooper who had accumulated a large gun collection. Linscott told the gang members the times when his sister would be away from her house. The gang stole the guns and the woman's jewelry. Robinson said he interviewed Linscott regarding that burglary and offered Linscott a chance at immunity if he cooperated with the investigation and helped his sister get her jewelry back. Linscott asked for time to think about it, but he never cooperated, nor was he ever prosecuted, Robinson said.

There is another burglary-ring connection to Bill Wickline, the killer and drug dealer who was hiding out in the Hocking Hills at the time of the murders and who was a leader of a gang of young thieves specializing in drugstore burglaries. This is the same Wickline who, in an apparently deliberate move to go to prison for some chill-out, dry-out time, allowed himself to be arrested in 1983 during a drugstore burglary in Nelsonville, where McKnight was living.

Could the leaders of those crime rings have had the influence to manipulate the investigation?

Bob Smith said his investigation of the Warren Gang did not produce enough evidence to indict any local law enforcement officials on related corruption charges. However, he added, he strongly suspected the gang was protected. "Corruption was always a question in the case. How else do you go thirty years untouched, the way they did?" Smith said. In 1990, the Warren Gang leaders were indicted on burglary and racketeering charges. Paul Warren, who lived in Hocking County, died in state prison.

There was definitely a leak from the Hocking County Courthouse during the Warren Gang investigation. "The Hocking County Sheriff's Department and the Ohio Organized Crime Commission learned that someone within the HCSD apparently was leaking information concerning these investigations," stated Magistrate Judge Stephen Kemp, in his ruling on a 1993 civil suit that pitted the leaders of the Johnston-Schultz murder investigation against each other. In that suit, Jim Thompson and other local police officers sued Sheriff Jimmy Jones for making covert tapes of phone calls in his office. The chief witness for the plaintiffs was Lanny North, Jones's chief deputy, who later succeeded Jones.

Judge Kemp ruled that Jones "acted in a wanton, reckless, or malicious manner" in making secret recordings of phone calls, actions that were "without any semblance of authority and under circumstances where he knew his actions to be illegal." The ruling also stated that Judge Kemp found North's testimony to be more credible than Jones's. The plaintiffs were each awarded $11,000 in compensatory and punitive damages.

The internal rifts within the local law enforcement community were not publicly visible at the time of the cornfield murders. Cooperation was the keynote, and there was a strong façade of unity in the designation of Dale Johnston as the sole suspect. The totally errant nature of that assumption allowed McKnight and Linscott to escape the original dragnet. In fact, both men were comfortable enough, and brazen enough, to remain quite close to the scene of their crimes. Linscott stayed right in his parents' house, a two-minute walk from the cornfield. He even went back to the cornfield to try to kill himself. He continued to deal drugs throughout most of those years, police now believe, and his own daughter died from a drug-trafficking-related overdose.

Chester went away briefly but then moved back to his old hometown about fifteen miles downriver from Logan. He committed at least two crimes with stark similarities to the Logan case, assaulting young women who were walking the railroad tracks near trestle bridges. Nobody with a badge made the connection, even though the first of those assaults occurred before Johnston was indicted in Logan.

Why didn't they run? They had participated in the most brutal murders in the history of Hocking County. Every step of the investigation was highly publicized. They knew the community was terrified and was demanding the killers be brought to justice. Linscott also must have known that his neighbors suspected him and had given his name to the police. Why then did both of these men feel secure enough to continue to live in the area and to continue to be part of the local crime and drug scenes?

All the red flags were disregarded, but for what? Instead of taking the short, straight path to the truth, the original investigators took a tortured, crooked path to the conviction of an innocent man. They were somehow able to convince a three-judge panel that Johnston had forced Todd and Annette into his car, made a stop at Sarah's office so she could join him for the grotesque but somehow bloodless murder scene at the Johnston trailer, and then shuttled the carved-up corpses back to the cornfield in Logan.

Even if one takes the huge leap of accepting that Johnston could have made such a trip without being detected, the physical layout alone of the crime scene makes that assumption seem absurd. He would have had to carry more than 250 pounds of dead weight from the access road at the edge of the cornfield to the riverbank more than one hundred yards away, and then navigate about a quarter mile of sloping, rocky, and underbrush-choked riverbank just to get to the point where the torsos were dumped into the river. That walk is difficult for a man carrying just a fishing pole, not to mention a heavily burdened man with a documented history of back problems.

The only time the prosecution's theory of the crime was revealed in full was during Frederick Mong's closing argument at the trial. Mong said only that Johnston brought the bodies back to the area where they had last been seen alive. He offered no evidence or even a guess as to why Johnston went to all the additional trouble of dragging a feedbag, or bags, loaded with body parts from the riverbank, through the cornstalks, and to the burial site. Police had been operating under the theory that Johnston was somehow trying to suggest some occult involvement in the crime, but with absolutely no evidence to support it, the prosecutors were apparently too embarrassed to stretch their scenario to that extent. Mong had the chance to cross-examine Johnston on the stand and to pose questions that might have at least challenged Johnston, but Mong chose to avoid the issue.

So, the prosecutors never offered an explanation for the discovery of a significant piece of evidence—the feedbag found near the access road leading over the tracks. Their scenario implied that Johnston may have dropped it. However, they overlooked a much more plausible theory, one supported by eyewitness Janice Moyer. The feedbag might have come from someone in the caravan of vehicles she saw using that access road late at night. Judy Linscott and Chester McKnight both have stated that Tex Meyers was at Linscott's house when the group of four walked toward the tracks. Could Meyers and some friends have been recruited by Kenny Linscott to help with the body disposal? According to Jill Wolfery, Meyers had access at Animal Crackers to the exact type of feedbag found by the tracks.

Prosecutors flirted with using a cult angle in their scenario but decided against it. Police theorized that Johnston may have buried the body parts in the cornfield as a way of throwing suspicion onto a satanic cult, but they were leery of going down the cult road, even though they had done so before. In the mid-1970s, there had been a series of animal mutilations in the region, and both Chris Veidt and Jim Thompson had been unequivocal in labeling the incidents as the work of a cult. After the discoveries of the body parts, however, police were quick to discount any suggestions of cult involvement.

Johnston's defense also prepared to use a cult expert at trial, where he would have testified that he saw signs of the occult, particularly in the way the body parts were buried and in the pattern of wounds on Todd Schultz's torso. The expert was not called because defense attorneys assumed they had done a good enough job of demolishing the state's case.

The occult theme has remained an undercurrent in the case. After the conviction, Rodney Robinson walked the crime scene area with Dolly Shaner, a cult researcher from the Hocking Hills area. Shaner said she saw obvious signs of cult activity on the riverbank near where the bodies were dismembered, in the form of occult symbols hanging from a tree. Furthermore, Shaner said she had been approached a few years before the murders by a group of women from Logan, who told her that the cornfield and riverbank were well-known hot spots for cult gatherings. Bill Wickline was also described by several people as having been deeply involved in cult rituals.

Now that the case is closed, there is little chance these unanswered questions will ever be officially investigated—and there is every indication that the people of Hocking County would prefer it stays that way. Both Chester McKnight and Kenny Linscott were placed under oath in the same courtroom where Dale Johnston was convicted and were given the opportunity to confess their crimes in detail. Each said little or nothing. The only other person McKnight implicated in the crime was Kenny Linscott, and one reason he offered for giving up Kenny was that Kenny was dying anyway. At Linscott's sentencing hearing, the judge, a brother of the former prosecutor, actually advised Linscott to remain silent.

Ed Kallay, the former investigator for the Ohio attorney general, said he encountered a reluctance to embarrass the police who'd botched the original investigation so thoroughly. "Those guys [Hocking County authorities in the reopened investigation] were scared to death of what Jimmy Jones and the old regime politicians would think," Kallay said. "They didn't want to upset the apple cart." At one point, some of the Hocking County investigators actually expressed a desire to run the newly developed information past Jones, to keep him in the investigative loop, he said.

Rodney Robinson said he and Jim Powers encountered the same resistance. When they met with Larry Beal, the county prosecutor at the time, and told him and his investigator that they had found witnesses who could prove Johnston didn't commit the murders. Beal's immediate response was to say that the first order of business would have to be proving Johnston innocent, rather than proving someone else guilty. "At first, they didn't want to reopen the case," Robinson said.

And just as the people don't seem too interested in pursuing the whole truth, they also seem content to hold onto the old lies. There is a clear strain of thought that even if Dale Johnston did not commit the murders, he must have been guilty of something. If Johnston had committed the assaults on his stepdaughter, as the original investigators and prosecutors alleged, then "he deserved every day in jail he got," said Laina Fetherolf, the Hocking County prosecuting attorney. She said the five years Johnston spent on death row were a just punishment for the crimes that others reported Annette accused Johnston of. Fetherolf said this opinion was expressed as a private individual, not in her capacity as a public official, but she isn't the only one in Logan who feels this way. In 2011, when the author was in Logan doing research, he struck up conversations with two strangers, and both expressed the same sentiments as Fetherolf, using nearly the same words.

In a strictly legal sense, however, Johnston was charged with murder, not sexual assault. All of the testimony regarding those allegations was hearsay, which, according to the appellate court, should have never been allowed into the trial. Annette herself never reported the supposed assaults to authorities, even though she had been urged to do so by some of the same people who claimed to have heard her make the allegations. Nevertheless, Fetherolf said, the second-hand claims that Annette was a victim of sexual abuse should not be dismissed entirely.

Lanny North, the current Hocking County sheriff, acknowledged that the guilty pleas by McKnight and Linscott have cleared Dale Johnston, but he defended the actions of those who led the murder investigation back then. "I can see now that mistakes were made," North said. "But at the time, Dale was the most likely suspect." Besides, he added, "Dale made himself look guilty." North was the chief deputy sheriff during the original investigation, and along with Rodney Robinson, he conducted the first interview of Steve Rine, the prosecution's star witness. North and Robinson decided Rine's information was not relevant to the investigation, but after Jim Thompson had Rine hypnotized, Rine's information became vital to obtaining the conviction.

Those who led the error-filled investigation, prosecution, and trial of Dale Johnston are reluctant to acknowledge the magnitude of their mistakes.

Former Hocking County Sheriff Jimmy Jones refuses to concede that his original investigation sent an innocent man to death row. In a November 2009 interview with the author, Jones said he's not convinced that McKnight was the killer and Linscott his accomplice. "I don't buy it," Jones said. "Their story doesn't jibe with what I know about the case."

Jones suggested that McKnight might be lying to boost his status in prison from admitted sex offender to double murderer. He also thinks Linscott's guilty plea might have been motivated by a desire to obtain health care services from the state. (Linscott qualified for indigent medical care before and after his guilty plea.)

He did not rush to judgment against Johnston, Jones said. "It took me almost a year to believe Dale Johnston did it," he said. But by the time of the September 1983 indictment, Jones had become convinced by the accumulation of evidence, particularly the footprint near the riverbank, the traces of evidence dug up from the trash pit near Johnston's home, Johnston's insistence that he never carried a gun or knife, and Johnston's eerie visions in which he claimed to see Todd and Annette in a watery setting.

Mistakes may have been made during the original investigation, but most of those were attributable to the conduct of Jim Thompson, Jones said. "He [Thompson] screwed things up," Jones said. It was Thompson who became fixated on Johnston almost immediately, he said. Thompson "wanted to arrest Johnston the same night we found the bodies," Jones said. "And Johnston knew that Thompson was out to get him."

The extent to which the original investigators were fixated on Dale Johnston is confirmed in the case files of the late Det. Herman Henry, which were obtained by the author from the Ohio attorney general's office, via a Freedom of Information Act request. From the time the bodies were discovered until Johnston was convicted, the files show that Henry's efforts to find the real killers were rebuffed consistently.

It was Henry who first pursued the leads that pointed to Tex Meyers's involvement in the crime. On October 20, less than three weeks after the murders, Henry talked by phone with Bob Snyder, the Columbus Police Department detective who'd received a report from his sister Jill Wolfery about Meyers's suspicious actions. The next day, Henry and Logan Police Chief William Barron went to Columbus to talk further with Snyder. Henry considered the information significant, and he prepared a report on Meyers based on police files on him. Henry stated in his report that Meyers frequently walked the railroad tracks near where the bodies were found, was known to be "very hot-tempered," and had a history of breaking into houses. The report was sent to both the Logan Police Department and the Hocking County Sheriff's Office. Snyder later made a visit to the sheriff's office to reinforce his concerns regarding Meyers. No one involved in the investigation picked up on the information—no one except Det. Rodney Robinson. Even though Robinson tracked Meyers down, his efforts to convince the other investigators to consider Meyers a suspect were shot down personally by Sheriff Jones.

In August 1983, shortly before Johnston was indicted, Henry chased down another initially promising lead. According to Henry's case files, a source gave Henry the name of a possible suspect, a nineteen-year-old man who'd stated that he'd been present when Todd and Annette had been killed, that he knew the killers, and that he knew how and where the murders had happened. Henry reported the lead directly to Chris Veidt, the prosecuting attorney. Veidt told Henry to follow up on the tip and to report directly back to him. Henry found the young man in question and interviewed his relatives. The man turned out to be a mental patient, who was more than likely making up his story. Henry concluded that he should not be considered a suspect, but the handling of his information illustrates the elements of distrust and deviousness that characterized the investigation.

In late December 1983, a few weeks before Johnston's trial, Henry tracked down a lead that might have caused the prosecution to reconsider its theory of the crime—had it bothered to listen to him. Henry developed information about a picture of Annette and an unidentified man—not Dale Johnston—having sex in the bed of a pickup truck. Henry tracked the tip to a retired phone company employee named Ralph Wharton, who confirmed that he'd seen the picture. It was taken in the late summer of 1982, Wharton told Henry, by a friend of Wharton's who owned property near the Johnston's home. The friend, whom Wharton refused to name, told Wharton that he saw the couple pull into his clover field and start to engage in sexual intercourse; the friend took a Polaroid snapshot of them and then told them to leave.

The name of the man photographed with Annette was redacted from Henry's files. Whoever it was, though, the matter should have been of interest to the people who were in the final stages of preparations for a death penalty trial. Anyone who was having sex with one of the murder victims

should at the very least have been interrogated. Of course, had such an interrogation taken place, the prosecution would have been required to turn
over the details of that interrogation to Johnston's attorneys. The evidence of
Annette having sex with another older man would have conflicted with the
prosecution scenario featuring Johnston's purported jealousy over Annette's
relationship with Todd. It would also provide the defense with the name of
someone to subpoena for the trial, thus introducing another possible suspect
and a whole new theory of the crime.

There was, however, no trial testimony about the picture—but that wasn't
because Henry didn't try to make the prosecutors aware of it. The latest dated
entry in Henry's case files is for January 5, 1984. Henry went to the county
courthouse and then to Veidt's office, seeking to deliver his files, including the
account of the photograph. He stated that he couldn't find Veidt, but then he
got his case notes typed up and hand-carried them to Veidt.

The trial went on, though hardly anything that was presented as evidence
turned out to be true. Nevertheless, the verdict was accepted as the truth by
most people in Logan. Now though, the dramatically revised version of the
truth has been accepted as fact by the state of Ohio.

Two of the judges who handed down the guilty verdict are still living.
In recent interviews with the author, both said there seemed to them to be
more than enough evidence to support the conviction . . . at that time.

"If the three of us heard it [the case against Johnston] today, we'd have
the same verdict," said Michael Corrigan, who recently retired as a judge in
the Ohio Eighth Circuit Court of Appeals and still serves as a visiting judge
for that court. Corrigan said the element of the case he recalled most clearly
was the testimony of Louise Robbins, the forensic anthropologist. He said
he found her "extremely credible" and her analysis of the footprint in the
riverbank "quite compelling."

Corrigan said he was totally unaware that two other men had pleaded
guilty in connection with the deaths of Todd and Annette until informed
by the author in a 2010 interview. When further informed that Linscott had
been discounted as a suspect by police in the original investigation and that
his name never appeared in the case files, Corrigan said, "I'm shocked."

Judge Joseph Cirigliano, now retired from the bench and in private practice in Avon, Ohio, said the members of the three-judge panel in the 1984 trial of Johnston had no reservations about returning a guilty verdict. "At the conclusion of the trial, there wasn't any question in our minds. He was the killer. Any other three judges would have found the same thing," he said.

He, too, cited the expert testimony on the footprint as particularly damaging to Johnston. "The footprint testimony sticks in my mind. I absolutely thought she was credible," he said.

The fact that two other men have now pleaded guilty to the murders does not mean the prosecution's case against Johnston was unworthy of belief at the time, he said. "It wasn't a fantasy. There was hard evidence, and the evidence pointed to him [Johnston]," Cirigliano said.

However, all the hearsay evidence about Johnston's relationship with his stepdaughter, while it may have seemed relevant at the time, is irrelevant now, he added. Aside from that issue, he said, had the evidence against Kenny Linscott—his erratic behavior, the gash on his forearm, his statement to police, his call seeking information about the bodies—been properly assessed by the investigators and prosecutors, there would have been little chance of getting a grand jury to indict Dale Johnston.

During the trial, Cirigliano said, he felt uneasy about the sometimes macabre sentiments evident in the community. He said he received five threatening letters and one letter opposing the death penalty and illustrated by a ghoulish drawing of a man being electrocuted. "I was glad to get out of there," Cirigliano said.

The state's acceptance of the guilty pleas from McKnight and Linscott should remove any lingering doubt about Johnston's involvement in the crimes, Cirigliano said. "Hell, today he's innocent. That's all there is to it," he said.

Christopher Veidt, the Hocking County prosecuting attorney at the time of the murders and the trial, said he thought the case against Johnston was solid. "There was evidence presented to a panel of judges, and the evidence justified going forth at the time," said Veidt, who is now in private practice in Logan.

Asked about the prosecution's original scenario of the crime, Veidt said that was put together mostly by Frederick Mong, his assistant at the time, who died about three years ago.

In 2007, Veidt said, he was informed by state and local investigators that the case was being reopened. "I hope you have some hard evidence," he said he told the investigators. After that, however, "I was left out of the loop," Veidt said.

In a 2010 interview with the author, Veidt said he had not been briefed on the full details of the reopened investigation. "I have to accept that the system works. However, the way it occurred is bound to leave doubts in people's minds. The evidence at the time justified the proceedings against Johnston—the relationship with his stepdaughter, the nude pictures, the threats (presented during the prosecution's case at the trial) against the lives of the boyfriends of his stepdaughter."

The Schultz family has accepted the recently revealed facts—even though that meant letting go of almost everything they had believed for a quarter century about the death of their son and brother.

"It was like somebody took my little snow globe of life and shook it all up," said Kendra Schultz, Todd's younger sister.

When the prosecutors were ready to indict McKnight and Linscott for the murders, they invited members of the Schultz family to a meeting to show them the evidence that had been gathered against the two men. Greg Schultz, Todd's older brother, said he entered the meeting thinking, "Where'd they come up with this fairy tale?" But after the fifteen-minute meeting, he said, he was convinced that the new story was the true story. "They'd taken what I thought I'd known for twenty-five years and turned it around. I was convinced beyond a reasonable doubt," he said.

As the case progressed, the Schultzes became more upset with the way it was being handled. In December 2008, when the prosecutors accepted McKnight's guilty plea, McKnight made a statement in court but provided very few details of the crimes. Then, the prosecutors informed the Schultz family that they would likely bargain for a plea to a lesser charge in Linscott's case. Greg Schultz said the prosecutors expressed doubts that a conviction could be obtained, even if the murder charge was reduced to manslaughter. The family pushed the prosecutors to go to trial anyway, Greg said. "We just wanted the truth to come out. We didn't care if they lost the case," he said.

In the end, there was no trial—and very little truth that came out in court. The charges against Linscott were reduced to misdemeanors. Against the expressed wishes of the Schultz family, Linscott was not only allowed to remain silent about the crimes he'd escaped punishment for, he was coached to do so—*by the judge.*

"The first time around, we felt we got let down by the system. The second time around, it was the same thing," Greg Schultz said. "The first time, they got the wrong guy; the second time, they let one of the right guys go free."

Still, the abrupt reality shift has not wiped out the bitterness that some members of the Schultz family feel toward the Johnstons. Don Schultz said he believes the incest allegations helped make Dale Johnston a likely suspect, and Johnston did little to dispel the rumors. "He was trying to cover up his thing with Annette," Don said, adding that he was more than willing to see Johnston executed, even to do the job himself. "I was ready to shoot him like the dirty dog he was, but then, come to find out he didn't do it," he said.

Sandy Schultz recalled being convinced that Sarah was somehow complicit in the murders. After the trial, she said, she taunted Sarah a few times when she saw her in town, saying things like, "Have you done any butchering lately?" Now, Sandy said, she hasn't gotten to the point where she regrets those remarks, but she does concede that she should not have made them.

The Logan murders were studied as an example of how grave errors can happen in death-penalty cases by William Lofquist, now head of the sociology department at the State University of New York at Geneseo. He wrote a chapter entitled "Whodunit? An Examination of the Production of Wrongful Convictions" for the 2001 book *Wrongly Convicted: Perspectives on Failed Justice*.

"The case is a classic whodunit: a grisly double murder in a small town; the victims young, attractive, and about to begin their lives together; a sexually abusive stepfather; rumors of drugs and police corruption," Lofquist wrote. His study was conducted after Dale Johnston's release from prison but years before the confession and guilty plea of Chester McKnight.

The dismissal of the charges against Johnston raised the issue of the fairness of the original investigation, he wrote. "One could argue that Dale Johnston was the victim of a malicious prosecution," he wrote. "Nevertheless, confirming and linking these elements are substantial hurdles."

Lofquist made inquiries into Jim Thompson's background and handling of the case. "Thompson was an overzealous, highly moralistic, somewhat unstable figure said to have been adversely affected by his service in Vietnam," he wrote. "He believed that the crimes of popular imagination—rampant drug use and trafficking, child sexual abuse, and child pornography—were active threats in Logan. Quite plausibly . . . he became single-minded in his focus."

Nevertheless, Johnston made a likely suspect at the time, Lofquist wrote. Although Lofquist said he could not make a definitive after-the-fact finding on the credibility of the evidence presented by the footprint expert Louise Robbins, he could see in retrospect how Robbins's testimony could have been treated as credible at the time of the trial.

The guilty verdict, Lofquist concluded, was "the product of normal, day-to-day routine operations of decision makers acting free of conspiratorial intent or wrongdoing." That, in effect, was the "most disturbing" aspect of the case, he wrote. In other words, with the number of death penalty cases going through the justice system—particularly the ones where the defendant's guilt is at issue—errors of this magnitude are essentially inevitable.

"There is little reason to believe that the complex legal framework constructed around the death penalty has reduced the number of wrongful convictions or that further movement in this direction will produce a better result," he concluded.

In a 2011 interview with the author, Lofquist said it is legitimate to reraise the question of why the investigation became so tightly focused on Dale Johnston when there was evidence available at the outset pointing to the men who ultimately pleaded guilty to their involvement in the crimes. Finding the answers, however, may prove as difficult as it was in 1982, he added.

"I don't know where the line is between bad police practice and misconduct," he said.

The sordid, twenty-seven-year-long saga of the Logan murders is set in a small town in Ohio, but it offers insights into some of the deepest fears of Heartland America. During the 2008 presidential campaign, then-candidate Barack Obama caused himself quite a bit of trouble when he was quoted as criticizing people in small towns for clinging to their guns and their religion.

This case shows they cling to something much more basic. They cling to the notion that they are somehow removed and safe from the sorts of crimes they want to believe happen only in the big cities. They cling to the notion that they are somehow better in a moral sense than the people trapped in the urban jungles. They want desperately to be reassured that someone who could commit such terrible crimes could not be one of them, could not be their neighbor.

To preserve those illusions, the people of Logan were more than willing to send an innocent man to his execution. They cheered the shameful guilty verdict. The bitter irony is that, in doing so, they also ensured that the evil they feared would remain in their midst for twenty-seven years, festering and spawning more crimes.

Updating the key characters in this story:

Former Hocking Sheriff Jimmy Jones, whose work on the cornfield murders helped him get reelected to the second of his five terms as sheriff, is retired and lives in Hocking County.

Former Logan PD Det. Jim Thompson is a deputy sheriff in Athens County.

Former Prosecutor Christopher Veidt practices law in Hocking County.

Former Prosecutor Frederick Mong parlayed his victory in the Dale Johnston trial to a judgeship. He died in office as a respected jurist.

Kenny Linscott lives in a rent-subsidized apartment in Logan.

Chester McKnight will be eligible for parole in 2037; he would be seventy-nine then. He said he confessed to bring some closure to the family of the victims, but he also said he was hoping for some peace in his own heart. He has not found it. He said he is still haunted by his crimes. His bouts of depression took him to the point of planning to petition the state of Ohio to deliver the punishment once intended for Dale Johnston. "I just hope that when I send this letter to the governor that he will write the executive order for me to be put to death, and then the nightmares and their screams will stop forever," McKnight stated in a letter to the author.

Bob Suhr continues to represent Dale Johnston. On Johnston's behalf, he has filed a second wrongful imprisonment suit, naming the state of Ohio and Hocking Count as defendants. The defendants have opposed the suit on the grounds that Johnston has failed in earlier litigation to obtain compensation; thus, the governmental entities are protected under the concept of double jeopardy.

Michelle Cooper (she now uses her original surname) has a son, and she has recently moved from Colorado back to Ohio.

Sarah Johnston Brown (she now prefers that her maiden name be used) lives with her husband on his family's farm near the Ohio River, about fifty miles from Logan. The guilty pleas of the real killers have brought her little relief from the anger and bitterness that have consumed her. The way she and her family were treated has even overwhelmed her sorrow over the loss of her daughter. "I've never been able to grieve properly for Annette," Sarah says.

Dale Johnston lives with his wife in a modest home that he has made comfortable with his construction skills. They have a yard decorated by an array of flower beds. Just as God restored the biblical Job, he believes, he has gained much of what had been taken from him, at least in the material sense. He doesn't expend much energy dwelling on the pain from his losses, and he doesn't feel the need to convince anyone that he has been totally vindicated.

"If people are dead set on believing I killed somebody, that's not going to change—but that's their problem," Johnston said. "When an innocent person is sent to prison, it means the real perpetrators are still out on the streets. I wonder how some of those people feel now, knowing those creeps who killed Todd and Annette were living amongst them every day of all those years."

To this day, no one in authority at any level has apologized to Michelle, Sarah, or Dale.

NOTES

1. DEATH STROLL

Background information on Annette Johnston: Sarah Johnston Brown (mother), in discussion with author, June 1989. Dale Johnston (stepfather), in discussion with author, June 1989.

Background information on Todd Schultz: Sandra Schultz (mother), in discussion with author, June 1989. Sarah Johnston Brown, discussion, June 1989. Dale Johnston, discussion, June 1989.

Actions of Todd and Annette on day of their disappearance: *State of Ohio v. Johnston,* Hocking County Common Pleas Court (1984), Sandra Schultz Testimony 37–50; Don Schultz Testimony 28–32; Clara Anderson Testimony 565–70; Melody Morehouse Testimony 597–605; Scott Cauthen Testimony 581–97.

Reports of gunshots in the cornfield: *State of Ohio v. Johnston,* Hocking County Common Pleas Court (1984), Rebecca Troops Testimony 1351–54; Ruth Cullison Testimony 1340–51. *State of Ohio v. Johnston,* Court of Appeals of Ohio Fourth District (1986), Charles Bartow Affidavit; Shirley Frazier Affidavit. Shirley Frazier, in discussion with author, June 1989.

Strange noises from riverbank: *State of Ohio v. Johnston,* Court of Appeals of Ohio Fourth District (1986), Clarence Mason Affidavit.

Traffic in the cornfield: Janice Moyer, in discussion with author, June 1989.

Confrontation between Dale Johnston and Sandra Schultz, 10/05/82: *State of Ohio v. Johnston,* Hocking County Common Pleas Court (1984), Sandra Schultz Testimony 37–51; Dale Johnston Testimony 1570–1660, 1684–1726.

Johnston's efforts to find missing couple: Ibid. Dale Johnston, discussion, June 1989.

Search efforts and discovery of body parts: Ibid. *State of Ohio v. Johnston,* Hocking County Common Pleas Court (1984), James "Jimmy" Jones (Hocking County sheriff) Testimony 75–108; Charles Barron (Logan Police Department chief)

Testimony 51–74; Michael Downhour (Hocking County sheriff's deputy) Testimony 1481–1504.

Johnston's interview with police after discovery of torsos: Ibid. *State of Ohio v. Johnston,* Hocking County Common Pleas Court (1984), Dale Johnston Testimony 1570–1660, 1684–1726; Jimmy Jones Testimony 75–108; Steve Mowery (Hocking County sheriff's deputy) Testimony 292–355.

Police conduct at crime scene: Ibid. Herman Henry (Ohio Bureau of Criminal Investigation detective) Testimony 252–69. Herman Henry, in discussion with author, June 1989.

2. GUILTY BY POPULAR DEMAND

Interrogation of Dale Johnston: *State of Ohio v. Johnston,* Hocking County Common Pleas Court (1984), James "Jim" Thompson (Logan Police Department detective) Testimony 460–518; Steve Mowery Testimony 292–355; Herman Henry Testimony 252–69; Dale Johnston Testimony 1570–1660, 1684–1726. Dale Johnston, discussion, June 1989.

Background information on Dale Johnston: Ibid. *State of Ohio v. Johnston,* Hocking County Common Pleas Court (1984), Dale Johnston Testimony 1570–1660, 1684–1726. Dale Johnston, discussion, June 1989. Sarah Johnston Brown, discussion, June 1989.

Background information on Sarah Johnston Brown: Sarah Johnston Brown, discussion, June 1989. Dale Johnston, discussion, June 1989.

Sexual history of Annette Johnston and her relationship with Todd Schultz: Ibid. *State of Ohio v. Johnston,* Hocking County Common Pleas Court (1984), Sandra Schultz Testimony 1160–87; Sarah Johnston Brown Testimony 765–876. Sarah Johnston Brown, discussion, June 1989. Dale Johnston, discussion, June 1989.

3. THE SUBPRIME SUSPECTS

Background information on William Wickline: Bill Osinski, "Macabre Tale of Human Butcher Slayings Raises Suspicions about Inmate," *Akron Beacon Journal,* April 13, 1986. James Lanfear (Columbus Police Department detective), in discussion with author, March 1986.

Murders of Chris and Peggy Lerch: Theresa Kemp, in discussion with author, March 1986. *State of Ohio v. Wickline,* Franklin County Common Pleas Court (1985), Theresa Kemp Testimony 682–801.

Background information on Tex Meyers: *State of Ohio v. Johnston,* Ohio Court of Appeals Fourth District (1986), Jill Wolfery Affidavit. Jill Wolfery, in discussion with author, June 1989.

Efforts to have Meyers investigated: Wolfery, discussion. Bob Snyder (Columbus Police Department detective), in discussion with author, June 1989. Rodney Robinson (Hocking County sheriff's deputy), in discussions with author, March 2009, April 2010.

4. CARD-HOUSE ARCHITECTS

Initial police interview with Steve Rine: *State of Ohio v. Johnston,* Hocking County Common Pleas Court (1983), Rodney Robinson Testimony 1509–17.

Hypnosis of Steve Rine: *State of Ohio v. Johnston,* Hocking County Common Pleas Court (1983), Jim Thompson Testimony 619–32; Steve Rine Testimony 632–52, 717–32.

Visit to Logan by cult expert Dale Griffiths: Dale Griffiths, in discussion with author, March 2009.

Meeting with Thompson and member of religious sect: Jim Lanfear, in discussion with author, June 1989.

Efforts to discredit Dr. Mason: Ibid. *State of Ohio v. Johnston,* Hocking County Common Pleas Court (1983), Dr. Milton Mason Testimony 1412–34.

Alleged sighting of Johnston family at Mason's office: *State of Ohio v. Johnston,* Hocking County Common Pleas Court (1983), Eugene McDaniels Testimony 744–65.

FBI analysis of footprint on riverbank: *State of Ohio v. Johnston,* Hocking County Common Pleas Court (1983), William Bodziak (FBI agent) Testimony 732–44.

Footprint analysis by Louise Robbins: *State of Ohio v. Johnston,* Hocking County Common Pleas Court (1983), Louise Robbins Testimony 1207–1306.

Investigation of Robbins's testimony: CBS News, *48 Hours,* 1993.

Interrogation of Michelle Cooper: Michelle Cooper, in discussions with author, June 1989, March 2009.

Indictment of Dale Johnston: Bob Batz and Mark Fisher, "Stepfather Jailed in Teens' Slayings," *Columbus Dispatch,* September 30, 1983. Dale Johnston, discussion, June 1989. Sarah Johnston Brown, discussion, June 1989.

5. CARNIVAL OF COURTROOM CONFABULATION

State of Ohio v. Johnston, Hocking County Court of Common Pleas (1984), Herman Henry Testimony 252–69; Dr. Patrick Fardal Testimony 191–252; James Thompson Testimony 460–519; Annette Farley Testimony 523–36; Harold Sommers Testimony 551–65; Steve Rine Testimony 632–52, 712–32; Dr. Bruce Goldsmith Testimony 1366–1402; William Bodziak Testimony 732–44; Dr. Louise Robbins Testimony 1207–1306; Dr. Clyde Snow Testimony 1660–84; Michelle Cooper Testimony

901–78; Dale Johnston Testimony 1570–1660, 1684–1726; Frederick Mong (assistant prosecuting attorney) Closing Argument 1756–73; Debra Carter Testimony 1736–40; Robert Suhr (defense attorney) Closing Argument 1773–1805.

6. ONE CONVICTED, THREE SENTENCED

Dale Johnston, in discussions with author, March 2009, June 2009, November 2009.
Sarah Johnston Brown, in discussions with author, June 2009, May 2010.
Michelle Cooper, in discussions with author, July 2009, May 2010.

7. FREE IS A FOUR-LETTER WORD

Bud Walker, in discussions with author, May 1985, October 1985.
State of Ohio v. Johnston, Ohio State Court of Appeals Fourth District (1986), Ruling.
State of Ohio v. Johnston, Ohio Supreme Court (October 5, 1988), Ruling.
Efforts to retry Johnston: Charles Gerken, in discussion with author, October 2011.
    State of Ohio v. Johnston, Franklin County Court of Common Pleas, (1988), Judge
    William Gillie Ruling.
Johnston's release and reactions: Mark Fisher, "Man Who Spent 5 Years on Death
    Row Walks Free," *Dayton Daily News,* May 12, 1990.
Johnston's actions after release: Dale Johnston, discussion, March 2009.

8. CRACKING THE DAM OF LIES

Efforts to reopen case: Rodney Robinson, in discussion with author, October 2009,
    March 2010, May 2010. Jim Powers, in discussions with author, October 2009,
    March 2010, May 2010.
State participation in investigation: Ed Kallay (Ohio attorney general's office, for-
    mer investigator), in discussion with author, March 2010.
Initial statements of Judy Linscott: Judy Linscott, in discussion with author, May
    2010. Jim Powers, discussion, May 2010.
Investigative actions by Hocking County authorities: Matt Speckman (Hocking
    County, former chief sheriff's deputy), in discussion with author, May 2009.
    Case summary prepared by Matt Speckman, May 2009. Lanny North (Hocking
    County sheriff), in discussion with author, May 2009.
Chester McKnight statements: Chester McKnight, in discussions with author, March
    2009, October 2009. Case summary prepared by Speckman.
Response by prison officials: Patrick Fisher (Madison Correctional Institution in-
    vestigator), in discussion with author, October 2009.
McKnight's criminal record: Case files, Athens County Clerk of Courts, Records
    Division. Investigative file compiled by Ohio attorney general's office.

McKnight's polygraph examination: Case summary prepared by Speckman.

McKnight's plea hearing: Gretchen Gregory, *Logan Daily News,* December 19, 2008.

Interrogations of Kenny Linscott: Matt Speckman, in discussion with author, May 2009.

Powers, discussion, May 2009. Case summary prepared by Speckman.

Linscott's defense strategy: Kenny Linscott, in discussion with author, August 2009. Bob Toy (Linscott's attorney), in discussion with author, August 2009.

Linscott's plea bargain: Laina Fetherolf (Hocking County prosecuting attorney), in discussion with author, May 2009.

Linscott's plea hearing: Gretchen Gregory, *Logan Daily News,* June 18, 2009.

9. CHESTER AND KENNY

McKnight's childhood: Chester McKnight, in discussions with author, March 2009, October 2009. Chester McKnight, in letters to author, February 2010 to January 2012. Donna McKnight, in discussion with author, June 2010. Lorena Harkless, in discussion with author, March 2010. Allen Mohney, in discussion with author, March 2010.

McKnight's time of residence in Logan: Rusty Spence, in conversation with author, October 2010.

McKnight's police and prison record after Logan murders: Case files, Athens County Clerk of Courts, Records Division. Case file of McKnight investigation, Ohio Attorney General's Office. Court documents in Athens County. Chester McKnight, discussions.

McKnight's marriage: Chester McKnight, in letters to author, February 2010 to January 2012. Donna McKnight, in discussions with author, June 2010 and September 2011. Diana (McKnight's former wife), in discussion with author, August 2011.

Linscott's behavior at time of murders: Kenny Linscott, in discussion with author, June 2009. Rusty Spence, in discussion with author, September 2009. Judy Linscott, in discussion with author, March 2010.

Linscott's denial of guilt: Kenny Linscott, discussion, June 2009.

10. BLOOD ON THE CORN

Events at Linscott home: Judy Linscott, in discussion with author, March 2010. Chester McKnight, in discussion with author, October 2009, and in letters to author, February 2010 to January 2012.

McKnight's account of murders: Chester McKnight, in discussions with author, March 2009, October 2009, and in letters to author, February 2010 to January 2012. Case summary prepared by Speckman.

11. GUILTVILLE, USA

Warren Gang: Bob Smith (Ohio Organized Crime Commission, former director), in discussion with author, March 2010. Rodney Robinson, in discussions with author, October 2009, June 2010.

Warren Gang links to McKnight and Linscott: Kallay, discussion, March 2010. Rodney Robinson, discussion, June 2010. Case file of McKnight investigation, Ohio Attorney General's Office.

Investigative leak from Hocking County Sheriff's Department: United States District Court Southeast District of Ohio (June 28, 1994), Magistrate Judge Stephen Kemp Ruling.

Cult activity in Logan: Dolly Shaner, in discussion with author, June 2009. Dale Griffiths, in discussion with author, March 2010.

Reluctance of Hocking County authorities to reopen case: Kallay, discussion, June 2010. Robinson, discussion, June 2010.

Response to McKnight and Linscott guilty pleas: Laina Fetherolf, in discussion with author, June 2010. Jimmy Jones, in discussion with author, March 2011. Lanny North, in discussion with author, June 2010. Christopher Veidt, in discussion with author, June 2011. Judge Michael Corrigan, in discussion with author, March 2010. Judge Joseph Cirigliano, in discussion with author, March 2010.

Herman Henry efforts to investigate murders: Herman Henry, discussion, June 1989. Case file of Herman Henry's 1982 investigation of murders, Ohio Attorney General's Office.

Schultz family reactions: Sandra Schultz, in discussion with author, March 2011. Don Schultz, in discussion with author, March 2011. Greg Schultz, in discussion with author, March 2011. Kendra Schultz, in discussion with author, March 2011.

Reactions of Dale Johnston and Sarah Johnston Brown: Dale Johnston, in discussion with author, March 2011; Sarah Johnston Brown, in discussion with author, October 2010.

Lofquist study of Logan murders: William Lofquist, *Wrongly Convicted: Perspectives on Failed Justice*, ed. Saundra D. Westervelt and John A. Humphrey (New Brunswick, NJ: Rutgers University Press, 2001). William Lofquist, in discussion with author, June 2011.

Author's efforts to obtain interviews and comment from Jim Thompson: Written messages left at Thompson's office, calls to Thompson's office, and a certified letter sent to Thompson's office.

Linscott's informant status: Kenny Linscott, in discussion with author, January 2012.

INDEX

177